PRAISE FOR *BRAG!*

"Go ahead, make some noise! Brag master Peggy Klaus can show you how."
— *Working Mother*

"Klaus's approach is radical."
—Lynn Scherr, ABC TV's *20/20*

"Always on target. . . . Klaus provides solid advice."
— *San Jose Mercury News*

"Like a talk-show host, this petite powerhouse of a woman . . . is a show-don't-tell kind of teacher."
— *Christian Science Monitor*

"Klaus blows away the myths on bragging. . . . She gives practical, hands-on advice. . . . An indispensable book."
— *Texas Lawyer*

"Simple-to-understand, real-life concepts. . . . Her advice is golden; it provides the polished style and refined substance needed to climb the corporate ladder. Of all the books I have ever read, I found Klaus's to have the most grace and the most overall, long-term impact."
—Myshelf.com

"Masterful!"
— *Glamour*

"Klaus's persuasive writing style and authentic tone combined with real-life anecdotes show off the transformative effect successful bragging can have on a career."
— *Publishers Weekly*

more . . .

"Klaus shows you how to self-promote by sharing your passion and vision with grace and dignity, an all too rare occurrence in today's corporate environment. Packed with smart advice, BRAG! is a refreshing read for anyone at any level."
—Dr. John C. Maxwell, founder, The INJOY Group,
and bestselling author of
The 21 Irrefutable Laws of Leadership and *Thinking for a Change*

"Klaus briskly removes bragging from the list of deadly sins and sets it squarely among the corporate virtues. With pithy anecdotes and insight, she invites us to communicate our identity through well-timed, intelligent, and artful bragging. If this book jolts you into the recognition that bragging is necessary for survival, it is worth the price."
—Harry Kavros, associate dean, Columbia Law School,
and former COO, Global Economics and Fixed Income Research,
Credit Suisse First Boston

"BRAG! will change your life. . . . It did mine and so many others in our organization of successful female professionals."
—Dana Hall, managing director, CFA Lighthouse Partners, LLC,
founder and president of the board,
100 Women in Hedge-Funds, Inc.

"When it comes to developing personal publicity, BRAG! is a must-read."
—*Detroit News*

"Peggy Klaus, I think you've convinced a lot of us."
—Ann Curry, NBC TV's *The Today Show*

BRAG!

THE ART OF

TOOTING YOUR

OWN HORN WITHOUT

BLOWING

IT

PEGGY KLAUS

BUSINESS PLUS

NEW YORK   BOSTON

Business Plus
Hachette Book Group
237 Park Avenue
New York, NY 10017

www.HachetteBookGroup.com

Printed in the United States of America
Originally published in hardcover by Hachette Book Group.
First Trade Edition: May 2004
10 9 8

Business Plus is an imprint of Grand Central Publishing.
The Business Plus name and logo are trademarks of Hachette Book Group, Inc.

The Library of Congress has catalogued the hardcover edition as follows:

Klaus, Peggy.
    Brag! : the art of tooting your own horn without blowing it / Peggy Klaus.
    p. cm.
    ISBN 0-446-53179-0
    1. Self-presentation. 2. Interpersonal communication. 3. Success in business. I. Title.
    BF697.5.S44 K57 2003
    6501—dc21   2002191043

ISBN 978-0-446-69278-6 (pbk.)

Book design by Giorgetta Bell McRee

For my clients,
who have shared with me their best selves.
And for Robin,
who had so much to brag about.

ACKNOWLEDGMENTS

If someone had told me a year ago that I would write a book, I would have said "Oh, right, and I'm also going to dance with the San Francisco Ballet." At forty-eight and 5 feet 2 inches, it just wasn't going to happen. But then, life took an odd turn. Almost before I knew it, I had become "the Brag Lady," and people began asking for a book. So I wrote a proposal, found an agent who liked it, who found a publisher who also liked it, and suddenly, I was writing *Brag!*

From the very beginning, putting this book together was a team effort. I could not have done it without the help of two women, the very embodiment of the phrase "grace under pressure." To Jane Rohman, collaborator and publicist extraordinaire, my gratitude for your laserlike focus, constant creativity, and for "getting my voice" from the day we met. To Molly Hamaker, my collaborator in all things creative and corporate, my love and appreciation for letting me into your life at a time when you didn't have room for one more thing. Without you, neither this book nor my business would have taken shape. Thank you for being my guide, my friend, and my "sister."

To my parents, thank you for giving me the passion and the skills to make my way in the world. To my sisters and best friends, Kathy, Mary, and Nancy, thank you for being with me from the very beginning of my journey. Steve, Jeffrey, and Nelson you have added so much to our family, not the least of which has been six beautiful nieces and nephews. Ross, Zachary, Zoe, Max, Jacob, and Ani, thanks for being who you are and for sharing yourselves with me. I am so proud to be your aunt.

A big hug to my wonderful friends: the Elkins Park gang, the LA Winers, the Philly pals, and my West Coast "family." Amy Eisman, you are an angel for insisting that *Brag!* was the book I had to write. And Mary Mattson, thank you for knowing that Jane and I had to work together. You were brilliant, as always. Lois Barth, Melinda Leudtke, Robin Dorman, Bobbie Roth, Bob Riskin, Lynne Broadwell, Jonathan Bricklin, Trena Cleland, Tal Harrari, and my favorite father-in-law, Gerry Keyworth; you made me think I could do it. Thanks.

To Jamie Raab, an old friend long before she became my publisher, and her sweet husband, Dennis Dalrymple, thank you for feeding me home-cooked meals along with loads of encouragement to "write the damn book already." Had it not been for your nudging, I would never have even thought about writing a book.

To my agent, Jim Levine, thank you for having the courage to work with another Klaus. Not only are you brave, you've got great literary taste as well. To Rick Wolff, my very patient and reassuring editor, thank you for tak-

ing on this first-time author riddled with literary insecu-
rities. I would love to work with you again, but can I
please have a four-month deadline next time? And to my
fabulous copyeditor, Anne Montague, thank you for your
sharp eye and great suggestions.

I owe Joann Lublin a huge thank-you, because it was
her article about me in the *Wall Street Journal* that spurred
all this interest in bragging.

To everyone at K & A: Eric Strelneck, Tasha Bigelow,
Janie Rose, Jennifer Rodrigue, a big hug and many thanks
for putting up with me.

A special thanks to my many clients and friends whose
stories have been included in this book. (Don't worry: I've
changed names and details to protect your privacy.)

And finally, to my sweet husband, Randy Keyworth;
you believed in me long before I learned to believe in myself. For that and so much more, my deepest love, now and
always.

CONTENTS

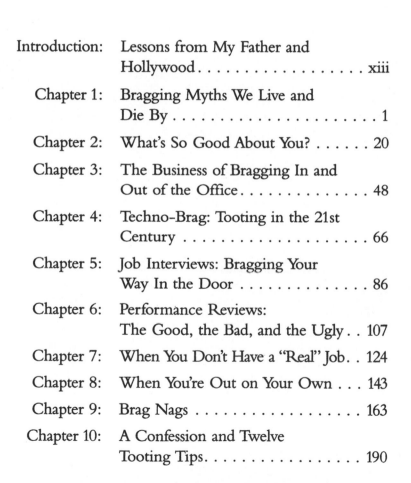

Introduction: Lessons from My Father and
Hollywood xiii

Chapter 1:   Bragging Myths We Live and
Die By 1

Chapter 2:   What's So Good About You? 20

Chapter 3:   The Business of Bragging In and
Out of the Office 48

Chapter 4:   Techno-Brag: Tooting in the 21st
Century 66

Chapter 5:   Job Interviews: Bragging Your
Way In the Door 86

Chapter 6:   Performance Reviews:
The Good, the Bad, and the Ugly . . 107

Chapter 7:   When You Don't Have a "Real" Job . . 124

Chapter 8:   When You're Out on Your Own . . . 143

Chapter 9:   Brag Nags 163

Chapter 10:   A Confession and Twelve
Tooting Tips 190

INTRODUCTION

◎

Lessons from My Father
and Hollywood

I will never forget when I was nine years old and won a tennis match against an older neighborhood boy, a star on the junior-high tennis team. I whooped and hollered, telling anyone who crossed my path about my big victory—until one day, my father overheard me. He pulled me aside and said, "Peggy, don't toot your own horn; if you do a good job people will notice you." It was to become a caution I heard often from my father while growing up in Philadelphia, enjoying a fair amount of success from my various pursuits. He had a tremendous influence on me, especially given that he was raising four girls on his own after our mother died. I took my father's message to heart and never tooted my own horn, not even casting a vote for myself for senior class president.

Then I grew up and went to Hollywood, the bragging capital of the world. All hell broke loose.

As I interviewed for jobs in the entertainment business, I quickly discovered I wasn't very good at talking about my accomplishments or myself. In fact, I had become my father's words. I was exceedingly self-deprecating, lacking the confidence and bravado others seemed to display so effortlessly. When put in the spotlight of explaining myself, I became racked with self-doubt. It was painful. In Hollywood, not only did you have to *think* you were the best, you had to be able to *say* it. And I *hated* it when people did.

One rejection followed another. My fear of becoming a bag lady was quickly replaced by the challenge of becoming the brag lady. How could I talk about myself in a way that felt natural and comfortable? How could I do so without coming off as arrogant, self-aggrandizing, or sounding like "one of them"?

We all have experienced "one of them"—those people who are walking billboards, flagrant self-promoters: a boss, a co-worker, your next-door neighbor, that guy at the cocktail party, or the kid on the playground so many of us remember. The ones who always elbow their way in, reminding you they are harder working, more accomplished, more deserving, and downright better than you. And then to really add insult to injury, they get ahead.

AN AH-HA MOMENT: THE VALUE OF A GOOD STORY

In retrospect, the way I overcame my reticence during interviews was quite simple: I started putting together what I now call a bragologue. It began by my writing down on paper a litany of everything I had accomplished, both personally and professionally. I then took the best parts of my life and wove them together, creating the Peggy Klaus

Story. I practiced delivering my tale with the same enthusiasm I used when telling friends about a recent adventure. I knew instinctively that if I couldn't get excited about my accomplishments, no one else would. There were just too many stories around competing for airtime.

When I started selling myself using this subtle and storylike approach, the results were immediate and amazing. Suddenly there was a real difference in the way my audience—agents, managers, casting directors, network executives, even my competition—responded. They sat up with ears perked. They not only wanted to listen to me, they asked for more. As my confidence grew, I found too that I didn't have to abandon my personality. I could toss in a little dry humor and even a few self-deprecating remarks. I didn't have to stop being myself. I could be warm *and* strong. I could have style *and* substance. *I could brag and get away with it!*

My newfound ability to promote myself, without becoming "one of them," helped me land a job. And although I went on to enjoy many more successes as a producer and director, that first Hollywood lesson was never lost: Success meant selling myself in a way that was not only persuasive, but uniquely me. During my stint in the entertainment industry, I found that many who failed to master the craft of self-promotion also failed to get the best parts. Called over after a phenomenal audition, the vast majority of actors turned into shrinking violets. When asked to tell me more about themselves, they found it hard to quickly articulate their achievements of the last year or so, much less from the span of a career. They didn't know how to weave their accomplishments into a convincing bragologue.

MORE THAN JUST A HOLLYWOOD HANG-UP

In 1993, I left the entertainment world to start my own communication consulting business based in Berkeley, California. When I began coaching professionals and executives in presentation skills, I was shocked to find that they, too, were also weak at self-promotion. People on all rungs of the corporate ladder—from entry level to middle management, from heads of divisions to heads of companies, from Silicon Valley to Wall Street—had a hard time talking about themselves. Most found it easier to display passion about their organizations, their products and services, their teams, their hobbies and families, or other individuals. In short, they were more likely to talk with enthusiasm about *anything but themselves*. When forced to take the spotlight, they tended to robotically recap their résumés like some PowerPoint presentation, relying on techniques learned from previous workshops or from well-meaning professors in "Presentation 101" college classes: "Just the facts, ma'am" or "Never put your hands in your pockets." Instead of being able to tell a client that they were responsible for doubling sales from $4 million to $8 million in six months, my clients spoke of their accomplishments in the vaguest of terms. Their fear of coming off as braggarts denied them the opportunity to relay the very information that would impress a prospective client.

Over the years, as my communication consulting expanded from platform skills to management and career issues, I started to cover self-promotion in my workshops and in one-on-one coaching sessions. My clients responded to me as if I were a dentist who had accidentally struck a raw nerve while drilling. *Brag* was clearly seen as a four-letter word. And by extension, the whole notion of self-promotion was excruciatingly difficult for professionals to embrace, even if they knew it was critical for their own survival. I made it my business to change their minds.

Promoting ourselves is not something we are taught to do. Even today, we still tell children "Don't talk about yourself; people won't like you." So ingrained are the myths about self-promotion, so repelled are we by obnoxious braggers, many people simply avoid talking about themselves. Two extremes. No happy medium. The problem (and the solution!) lies in our interpersonal communication skills. Not only are we uncertain about *what* to say about ourselves, we don't know *how* to say it with grace and impact in a way that's inviting to others.

GUYS HAVE THE EDGE . . . BUT EVEN THEY GET IT WRONG

In 2002, the *Wall Street Journal* devoted a column to my "Bragging Rites and Wrongs," a series of workshops about self-promotion I delivered to businesswomen across the country. The coverage resulted in an avalanche of response. My phone didn't stop ringing for weeks.

Many of the calls came from men. Why hadn't I included them in my workshops? Although I've coached an equal number of males and females, and find that bragging is difficult for both genders, the majority of women with whom I work struggle with this issue far more than men do. It's a well-researched fact that women are terrible self-promoters. Told by parents and society at large "Don't be a show-off," "Don't upstage your brother," "Don't talk about your accomplishments—it will make your boyfriend/husband look bad," women are less likely to draw attention to themselves and take ownership of their successes. They tend to attribute their accomplishments to other people, their families, or a work team. That's all very nice, but it's those who visibly take credit for accomplishments who are rewarded with promotions and gem assignments.

I often joke that men are born with the brag gene. But as one male remarked, "Oh no, it's not that we're born with this gene. We got it because by the sixth grade, we were already looking for dates. So we *had* to boast to separate ourselves from all the other boys." While men tend to brag more than women, and do so more comfortably, even they get it wrong. (Yes, more often than not, they are "one of them.") A common complaint I hear is that men alienate others by being too heavy on the "Me! Me! Me!" messages. Many also embellish their accomplishments to such an extreme degree—some call it flat-out lying—that it calls their credibility into question. (Certainly women can be guilty of this, too.) Some men have also grown up with the same self-limiting advice given to women. The response from men following the *Wall Street Journal* story convinced me that they are equally in need of bragging advice.

BRAGGING IS AN ART

The purpose of this book is not to teach you to make a lot of pretentious noise. It's to teach you to master the art of bragging, using the same techniques that have turned the thousands of professionals and executives I have coached into skillful self-promoters.

But for most of us, mastering the art of bragging is easier said than done. The problem we have with self-promotion is this: We think it's necessary to choose between remaining obscure or sounding obnoxious, like "one of them." Fortunately there is a bragging middle ground—an artful way of communicating and turning the spotlight on yourself that will not only feel natural and comfortable to you, but to those on the receiving end as well.

At its core, bragging is a very individual form of self-expression and communication. A good self-promoter sneaks up on you, grabs your attention, and wins you over—without your even knowing he or she is doing it. Good self-promoters have a way of connecting with others. They exude a contagious energy, coming off as confident about where they have been and where they are going. They know their stuff. Before even uttering a word, they take the emotional temperature of an audience, whether facing one or a few hundred. They speak with sincerity from both head and heart. They are exceptional storytellers, because they continually work at keeping their stories fresh. They're able to think on their feet, because they're always well prepared. They are masters at turning negatives into positives and are often funny, even self-deprecating at times. But most important, and this is key, they express themselves best by being themselves. Conveying authenticity is at the heart of good self-promotion. This book will teach you how to become a master of artful bragging.

HOW THIS BOOK WORKS

You are living in the Age of the Entrepreneur, even if you don't work for yourself. The workplace is no longer a safe and secure haven for anyone or any career—job security is virtually nonexistent. People are shedding jobs and careers at an unprecedented rate. The only sure thing is that no one is going to look after your best interests except you. And if you don't speak up for yourself, who will? Jobs and bosses will come and go. So the best way to thrive in this environment is to start thinking like an entrepreneur and to start bragging about your most valuable product: *you!*

Good self-promotion starts with recognizing and reconciling the myths that keep you from talking about yourself and realizing your goals. Chapter 1 covers these myths, showcasing missed opportunities and the value of tooting your own horn with examples of good and bad bragging dialogues.

Are you one of those people who can only think of the right things to say about themselves *after the fact?* Then read on.

Good self-promotion is very individualized, and one-size-fits-all solutions don't work. In Chapter 2, you'll find my "Take 12" questionnaire, a self-evaluation tool keyed to helping you unearth your personal and professional history, identify your strengths, accomplishments, and personality traits, and zero in on the things that make you *you*. I'll introduce you to the concepts of brag bites and bragologues, memorable sound bites and brief marketing monologues about yourself that can be drawn on in a moment's notice—and used to your advantage—in any situation without coming off as pushy or disingenuous.

Most of the remainder of the book is devoted to demonstrating how you can connect the dots to develop a unique and effective communication style best suited to your particular situation. Filled with tales of real-life bloopers and home runs, these chapters will show you how to translate your story into easy-to-use brag bites and bragologues that will successfully promote you wherever you go.

Chapter 3 focuses on the basics of business bragging in and out of the office. It's filled with schmoozing and cruising stories from the corporate world that show you how to maximize every encounter from elevator fly-bys to conversations with higher-ups at networking events to dealing with credit theft, which runs rampant in the corporate world.

Chapter 4 shows you how to use the latest technology to further your cause—how to harness voice mail and e-mail for "techno-brag" when dealing with clients or with colleagues and bosses who are away from the office. This chapter addresses the challenges and opportunities of being kept in mind when out of sight or off the site.

Chapters 5 and 6 focus on turning job interviews into job offers and performance appraisals into promotions and salary increases. With more people in and out of the workforce for a variety of reasons, Chapter 7 is dedicated to those without "real" jobs who want to leverage networking as well as casual cocktail chatter to plant seeds for future opportunities. Chapter 8 provides examples of using your personal history to give your company credibility or to obtain funding when you've decided to brave it on your own.

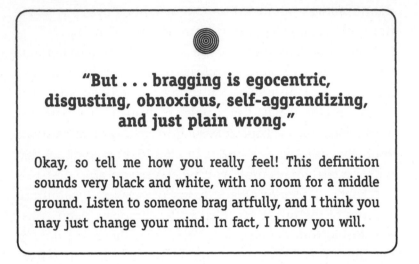

"But . . . bragging is egocentric, disgusting, obnoxious, self-aggrandizing, and just plain wrong."

Okay, so tell me how you really feel! This definition sounds very black and white, with no room for a middle ground. Listen to someone brag artfully, and I think you may just change your mind. In fact, I know you will.

Before you hit the bragging trail, dump everything you ever learned in Presentation 101! Chapter 9 teaches you my trademark "brag nags"—key communication techniques that make for more dynamic bragging in any situation and with every audience. You'll learn how to take the emotional temperature of the listener, how to be authentic at all times, and why you need to act like your best self, even on rainy days.

Chapter 10 wraps it all up with a humorous author's confession and, before I send you on your way, my Twelve Tooting Tips.

Once you learn to apply the techniques that have transformed my clients over the years, you'll see bragging in an entirely new light and discover a way to sell yourself that doesn't set you back, but actually sets you free.

Happy bragging!

Peggy Klaus
Berkeley, California
October 2002

FAST-FORWARD FIVE YEARS

When BRAG! was first published in 2003, reporters asked me why on earth I wrote a book about something that would turn everyone into obnoxious, self-aggrandizing bores. Did I really think Americans needed to brag more? It took some convincing for them to grasp that people are as likely to be ineffectively humble as overly braggadocios and that my book teaches a graceful way to self promote— yes, to brag—without looking and sounding like a walking billboard. Since BRAG! was released, self promotion has become more critical than ever with mergers, down-sizing, and bosses too busy to think about the professional development of their employees. Still, who could have guessed that, within five years, BRAG! would end up being printed in five languages, that companies worldwide would want hundreds of workshops on the topic, and that I would be called a bragologist? Even the biggest skeptics have finally come around—knowing how to "toot your own horn without blowing it" has become accepted as a must-have career skill!

Peggy Klaus
Berkeley, California
March 2008

Bragging Dictionary

Brag: To talk about your best self (interests, ideas, and accomplishments) with pride and passion in a conversational manner intended to excite admiration, interest, and wonder, without pretense or overstatement—in other words, without being obnoxious.

Brag bites: Snippets of impressive information about one's best self, expressed in a brief, quotable manner. They function as memory insurance so that people will remember something compelling about you. They can be dropped into conversations as single gems or woven together to create longer bragologues.

Bragologues: Ranging from a thirty-second elevator pitch to a three-minute monologue, information about one's self that is conveyed in a conversational, storylike fashion that's memorable and elicits interest, excitement, and/or admiration.

Brag bag: A collection of all the information about one's best self that can be easily accessed: accomplishments, passions, and interests—the colorful details that describe who one is personally and professionally.

Brag bomb: A complete failure in tooting one's own horn, typically a result of misreading one's audience, bad timing, and/or a lack of preparation.

Brag nags: Friendly advice on how to deliver your bragging with style.

Bragging "buts": All the excuses and issues that are cited as reasons for not bragging.

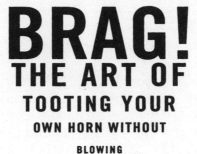

BRAG!
THE ART OF
TOOTING YOUR
OWN HORN WITHOUT
BLOWING
IT

CHAPTER 1

———————————◎———————————

Bragging Myths
We Live and Die By

It ain't bragging if you done it.
—Dizzy Dean

Myth #1:
A JOB WELL DONE
SPEAKS FOR ITSELF

It's not my father's workplace anymore, or even the one many of your mothers may have entered in the 1970s or '80s. The days of job security in exchange for loyalty and hard work are long gone. For most, this isn't news. Yet many of us fail to recognize the value of self-promotion in maneuvering today's volatile and unpredictable workplace. Given the constant changes—mergers, management shifts, downsizing—you simply must let people in the organization know who you are and what you are accomplishing. Otherwise you'll be passed over for promotions,

in succession planning, or when the company is determining the best performers during layoffs.

Even if you're an ace at keeping your boss up to speed,
remember, he or she might be gone tomorrow. You need
to cover all your bases and stand out in the eyes of your
boss' boss and that boss' boss and all the bosses right up to
the big boss. Your mission is made even more challenging
when you consider what the Information Age has
wrought: people who are overwhelmed by the daily on-
slaught of e-mails, voice mails, faxes, phone calls, and
meetings upon meetings. They have little-to-no time or
any real need to pay special attention to you.

Planting for the Future

As important as those on the inside of your company are
for your survival, those on the outside are just as significant: recruiters, industry associates, personal friends and
acquaintances, even your competitors. Even seemingly sta-
ble companies can collapse overnight. Just look at Enron
and Arthur Andersen, among many others.

Good self-promoters know this: They're always planting
seeds for the future. Karen, forty-two, a division head for
a major global food corporation, is a good example. At an
informal gathering, when asked how long she had been in
the business and what she did, instead of the typical "I've
worked with my company for fifteen years and run its
dairy division," she responded:

Who ever thought I'd be in the food industry, especially after my mom forced me all those years to eat Cheez Whiz? [Everyone at the table erupted with laughter.] It must have been fate, but after I graduated with my MBA from Columbia, I got a call from a friend who told me about a few interesting openings. I began working for my company in 1985 in brand management, working my way up to marketing director. Two years ago, one of the company's other divisions was really in the hole and they gave me the assignment of turning it around. I didn't really know where to start, so I began talking to people on the floor. A lot of them had great ideas. From there, I got everyone involved and formed teams to pull in the various disciplines and put together a strategic vision. Today, I am the proud head of a dairy division that is number two in profitability worldwide.

Smart self-promoters show up prepared. They value face time with others and are always ready with stories about themselves that break through the verbal clutter. They know that positive regard from others isn't going to "just happen" on job interviews, at performance appraisals, during presentations, or at networking functions. And it's unlikely to "just happen" by marching into the CEO's office and asking for an appointment to discuss how wonderful you are. It's not going to happen unless you make it happen, and the crème-de-la-crème opportunities to self-promote are going to come your way when you least expect them.

Myth #2:
BRAGGING IS SOMETHING YOU DO DURING PERFORMANCE REVIEWS

April 5, 2002: I am on a plane bound from New York to San Francisco and the thirty-something guy sitting next to me just blew it: He missed a golden opportunity to sell himself and his company.

We had struck up a conversation and were happily chatting away about living in San Francisco when I asked him, "So what is it that you do?" "I'm a management consultant," he replied. He didn't continue, so I tried to engage him more by asking, "What's your specialty in management consulting?" "Telecommunications," he responded, followed again by dead silence. I took on the exercise of seeing if I could pull out some more information asking, "Who do you do it for?" He named one of the top five management-consulting firms, then stopped cold. I was just about to ask another question when something inside me snapped. I thought to myself, I'm not asking a fourth question. I've done enough digging. He's not making it interesting or fun for me to talk with him.

Missed Opportunities

The first response from many clients hearing about this casual airplane encounter is to rattle off possible reasons why this fellow wasn't more forthcoming. Maybe he was tired, or reluctant to start tooting his own horn on an airplane, afraid that he might divulge sensitive information to prying ears, possibly a competitor's.

"But . . . in my culture bragging is a big no-no."

I understand and truly respect your cultural mores and traditions. Yet I think there is some wiggle room in all cultures. I'm not asking you to talk about yourself like you've called in an American marching band. Bragging in my book is subtle and seamlessly works its way into social and business interactions. If you do it right, they won't know what hit them.

While sometimes that may be true, in this case we were already *having* a conversation. So the point is, the road traveled by a lackluster self-promoter is paved with missed opportunities. You need to act like your best self even with strangers on airplanes and even when you don't feel like it. Before you quickly slam shut the book claiming *this* is exactly the reason you didn't go into sales, consider the following: Mr. Telecommunications didn't know who I was. I might have been a CTO of a company that could have used his consulting services. I might have been a recruiter who could come in handy one day when he'd gotten axed or one who was currently placing a specialist in the hottest new company in Silicon Valley. He didn't know that, in fact, I am a consultant who works with Fortune 500 firms and could possibly introduce him to an executive of a company that could have become a major new account. He never found out.

I wasn't asking him to reveal the location of the Holy Grail. I was simply asking that he tell me more about himself. If he had engaged me and talked about what he did and got me excited about it, I might have been a good future contact. I might have handed him some business. At the very least, *I would have remembered his story*.

Myth #3:
HUMILITY GETS YOU NOTICED

I've gone to spend a few days with my friend in the hinterlands of western Massachusetts and I find myself in an unlikely place: a tae kwon do class that her five-year-old son is enrolled in. The grand master, a Korean black belt, begins the class by asking the students to recite in unison the five themes by which to live. Lined up in military-style precision, each child exhibiting impeccable posture, they shout:

Self-control!
Honesty!
Perseverance!
Honor!
Humility!

There it is. That last one. Don't brag about yourself. Stating your value and accomplishments is risky because you might come across as pompous or make other people feel uncomfortable. It's safer and much more appealing to be humble and understated. But will you get ahead?

Humility is a virtue with biblical and spiritual roots that is taught the world over. In some areas of the world, such as Asia, humility is prized much the way we in America prize our freedom of speech. Early on we are taught humility for good reason. We haven't developed the social skills to talk about our accomplishments and ourselves gracefully. Instead, as children we blurt out, "My daddy has lots of money," "I'm better than you because . . ." or in the case of my friend's son, "I have more land than anyone," which he proudly proclaimed one morning between mouthfuls of Cheerios as his mother cringed. Our parents and mentors know it's important to squelch this behavior right from the get-go or people aren't going to like us. And they're right.

But the problem is this: Very few of us ever learn how to reconcile the virtue of humility with the need to promote ourselves in the workplace. When education and training do focus on selling ourselves, we're taught to pay the greatest care and attention to our wardrobe, our hair, our hygiene, our table manners, and our résumé. Get those things right, it's a slam dunk! There's very little instruction on selling ourselves with ease and sincerity. Somehow we think if we personalize our message or get too excited, we are not being professional, when in fact this is exactly what makes us effective self-promoters.

Wimping Out

The tug-of-war between showing humility and showcasing our accomplishments is played out daily across working America, even in the brashest of industries. Recently,
while conducting a workshop at a major Wall Street investment bank, I asked a group of young men and women
to update me on any successes they had experienced since
we'd last met when we worked on crafting more compelling sales pitches.

From the back of the room, I overheard one guy en-
couraging Patty, a twenty-six-year-old, perfectly coiffed
junior banker to share her success story. Even though she
had just landed a $10 million account, Patty seemed reluc-
tant. With prodding from the whole group, she finally
stood up. With her eyes directed toward the floor, her
shoulders shaped like an orangutan's, and in a whispery
voice that barely rose above the white noise of the conference room, she said:

> Oh, well, it's really nothing. It was a team effort.
> There was this guy who I had read about in the
> paper, so I wrote him and later called his assistant,
> who said he wanted to meet with me. I went in and
> told him about the services of the bank and what we
> could do for him. He said it sounded interesting and
> asked where do we go from here? And I said, well,
> I'll bring the portfolio manager and my senior banker
> with me and we'll make an appointment. So we went
> back in two weeks. I led off the meeting, but the se-

nior person did most of the talking, and we got a call yesterday and he's giving us ten million dollars.

And then she sat down.

I asked the group for some feedback. The fellow who had initially urged her on was flabbergasted. "Patty, what was that? You heard about this guy, you called him up, you met with him, and he gave you ten million dollars! You told it as if you had nothing to do with it. Quite frankly, you sounded like a wimp."

Patty replied, "Yeah, well, you know, a lot of people helped out. I didn't want to sound like I was bragging and taking all the credit."

An Ah-Ha Moment for Patty

Seeing that Patty was missing the point, I encouraged this co-worker to get up and act as though the story had happened to him. He said:

Oh man, I read about this guy in the paper. I got really excited about it. I wrote him a fabulous letter. I called his assistant to set up a meeting with him. On the day of the appointment, I was nervous but we still had a great conversation. I was really on my game that day. And he said, "What's the next step?" And I said, "I'll come back with my boss and portfolio manager. You're going to love them." When we walked in two weeks later, I introduced everyone to set the stage. Then they did their thing. Just yesterday the guy contacted me to give us his ten-million-dollar account. I am so psyched! I nursed this baby from beginning to end.

I asked the group to describe differences between the two versions of the story. The remarks were revealing: "David really owned it. He came across as excited about what happened. But he seemed authentic, too. He didn't come off like he was stretching the truth. You could tell he was really proud of what he had done."

Patty said, "Now that I've seen him do it and people respond so positively, maybe it wouldn't feel as uncomfortable to promote myself in this way." Like so many others I have coached, Patty was learning to overcome the whispers from her past, those similar to my father's, like "You're going to break an arm, patting yourself on the back too much."

Myth #4:
I DON'T HAVE TO BRAG;
PEOPLE WILL DO IT FOR ME

It's great if someone says something nice about you, but don't hold your breath. Although letting others do the bragging for you is one tool in your goody bag, it isn't your only tool. And it's no substitute for *you*. No one is going to have your interests at heart the way you do. No one will ever tell your story and get people excited about you like you can. Plus, nine times out of ten, when those to whom you report talk positively about your work to others, it's usually because there is something in it for them. Unfortunately, the accolade is often framed in such a way as to bolster them, more than you!

"But . . . maybe if I just brag about others, they'll brag about me."

I hear this one a lot, and there is some merit to what I call "quid pro-mote." Yes, it's great to acknowledge the accomplishments of others and hope that it's reciprocated. But make sure that when others talk about you, they say what you want them to. And never count on this as your only bragging avenue—many people feel as uncomfortable bragging about others as they do bragging about themselves.

Since most people rarely acquire the skills to promote and talk about themselves, many come to rely on others to do the dirty work and boast on their behalf. As children, most of us have at least one adoring fan who pushes us along, builds our ego and self-esteem: a parent, a coach, a favorite aunt or grandparent who takes us under a wing, or a teacher who's convinced we're the next Einstein or Michael Jordan. Where we start to really stumble is when we grow up. When we no longer have our childhood cheerleading squad on hand, many of us wrongly presume

that others in the workplace will fill their shoes and continue with unconditional support for our accomplishments
and us. And even then, when someone occasionally sings
our praises to others, we tend to deflect the compliments
with self-deprecating comments: "Oh, no, it wasn't anything," or like Patty, in the preceding example, "It wasn't
me. It was really the team."

Looking Out for #1

Bill, age twenty-one, a quiet, understated, no-nonsense
type of guy, has yet to grasp the most basic rules when it
comes to self-promotion. He's a go-getter salesman who
has just placed first in the Southwestern division for selling more of his company's software than anyone. He believes that his numbers speak for themselves and he
assumes that his boss, who has praised him often for his
sales prowess, will let the higher-ups know.

When his boss presents his division's sales results and es-
timates to senior management, here is what he says: "We've
had an excellent first half; we are up twenty-five percent,
a remarkable feat considering the tech downturn." When
asked by the CEO what's working, Bill's boss replies, "I've
put a top-notch sales force in place and I've trained them
well. You know that problem we were having with our
fixed-pricing schedule? Well, I sat down with Fred, the
marketing director, and we determined that if we allowed
our sales guys some greater flexibility and let them cus-
tomize some of the pricing—within limits, of course—

we'd sell substantially more units. And that is exactly what happened."

When someone mentions that she heard about Bill getting the award for the most sales in the Southwest, his boss says, "I knew the day he walked in that I could whip him into shape. I worked hard to get him on board, and it's paid off."

Even though Bill got the sales award, the boss took most of the credit. Bill's lackluster bragging skills limited him on two levels. First, because he placed very little importance on making personal connections with his boss or senior management, they had no vested interest in him, other than some guy making his numbers. Second, Bill's tight-lipped "sales are the only thing that matters" mentality is shortsighted. Had he revealed something more about himself and his story, his boss would have learned that Bill is from a tough neighborhood. He put himself through school and now spends a lot of his leisure time as a mentor with troubled youth. Knowing this, his boss might have told the CEO instead, "I knew the day he walked in that Bill was gold. He had already worked his way through college, and that kind of can-do attitude has paid off." Now, suddenly an image of Bill appears in everyone's mind. He becomes more than just a good hire. He becomes a gutsy, hardworking guy with a can-do attitude. And if Bill had mentioned to his boss his work with youth, a seed might have been planted. One of the higher-ups in the meeting asks Bill's boss if he knows of anyone who might be interested in starting a high-profile community outreach program to enhance the company's

image. Bill's boss says, "Not off the top of my head," and
Bill misses another golden opportunity.

Seldom are we encouraged to bring our background,
our experience, and our enthusiasm to the table and weave
them into a compelling human-interest story. It's ironic
that with all the advances in communications technology,
our interpersonal business communication skills languish
in the Dark Ages.

Myth #5:
MORE IS BETTER

It's a beautiful California morning. I am in my office early
when the phone rings and I answer it. Immediately I am
once again reminded that self-promotion is all about the
quality of one's message and story, rather than a boring list
of accomplishments. As the following discussion so vividly
demonstrates, it doesn't matter what you've done; if you
can't sell yourself in a way that's inviting to others, people
shut down.

"Hi, is Peggy Klaus in?" asked a female voice.

"Yes, this is she."

Never stopping to ask if this was a good time to talk,
this stranger proceeded to launch into a litany of her accomplishments, delivered with the precision of a Power-
Point presentation.

"I am so excited to talk to you. I just graduated with a
degree in communication. I was an excellent student with
a 4.0 GPA. I wrote for the school newspaper, which has

won accolades from all over the state. I also interned at a local advertising agency during the summers for the last four years. I have a very good reputation and references. For my term paper, I wrote about the changing role of communication in our society today. I think I would be perfect for a job in communication, and since you are involved in that, I wanted to speak with you."

I said, "I'm sorry, what was your name?"

She stated her name, but before I could get another word in edgewise, to my utter amazement, she continued: "I also forgot to tell you, I don't know how I could have forgotten, because it's so important, but I can't begin work for another month because I won a prestigious service award and will be traveling to Africa next month to help needy children."

I finally had to say, "Excuse me, Sarah. Obviously you've done so many things, but I have to tell you that I am not looking to hire anyone at this point. You might want to consider some of the larger firms in the area."

"Thank you for talking to me," she responded meekly, sounding as if the air had seeped out of her overinflated balloon.

Sarah, like many, is a victim of a one-size-fits-all method of presentation that emphasizes form over authenticity. (This is something I will explore more fully in Chapter 9.)

If she had only started off by asking, "Is this a convenient time to talk?," by telling me how she had learned about my firm, and by engaging me in a thirty-second story about herself, the result would have been different. Even though I wasn't hiring, I would have offered her the

name of a personal friend who was. As it was, I just
wanted to get her off the phone.

Myth #6:
GOOD GIRLS DON'T BRAG

I'll never forget the national television images of thirteen-
year-old Rebecca Sealfon, winner of the National Spelling
Bee, screaming and leaping around the stage in triumph of
her hard-won victory. Unlike Patty, the junior banker who
resisted telling others about her multimillion-dollar business win, Rebecca was excited and proud. She was happy
and confident. She was a female thrilled to tell the world
about her success.

She was one of the few.

Many talented women today continue to abide by the
myth that it's unbecoming and aggressive to promote
themselves. Although their parents may have told them
they could do anything they wanted, there was also a big
but. And that was, *but* don't celebrate your own glory. It
was all right if the boys vied for the limelight and one-
upped each other, but girls were taught to share it with
others. And even then, it was best not to draw too much
attention to themselves.

This disinclination among professional women to self-
promote has far-reaching consequences. It can affect referrals, negotiations of work schedule, salary, high-visibility
assignments, and promotions, as well as make your blood
boil when you see the guys getting ahead faster.

"But . . . the Bible says that modesty is a virtue."

Look, I'm not knocking the Bible or modesty, but as the old saying goes, "The Lord helps those who help themselves."

Showing Off Your Real Stuff

Throughout the years, I've worked with many female clients on changing the behaviors that result from the fear of upstaging male colleagues. Once I coached a physician from Harvard who was preparing a presentation to a large conference of her peers. Although only in her thirties, she had a tremendous amount of credibility in her field and a great deal of experience speaking at conferences. Yet when she practiced her presentation in my studio, she didn't come across as an assured, confident academic and scientist. Instead, she rambled, didn't appropriately introduce herself or her credentials, lacked a sense of urgency and excitement about her new breakthrough, and suppressed all of the delightful personality and sense of humor she had revealed in our earlier conversation.

When I asked about her style, she told me she didn't want to appear "too big" or "too braggy." She was concerned that her achievements would make her older and mostly male colleagues feel uncomfortable. What she did as a result was to present an unconvincing and boring recitation of her findings.

Fortunately, when she saw her performance on video playback in my studio, she didn't like what the tape exposed. She decided that she was willing to take the risk of stepping into the spotlight to present a fuller, more authentic version of herself. This didn't translate into acting "more like a man" or changing her personality. Instead, she learned to present her own characteristics with conviction and confidence by using direct eye contact, a sense of humor, and a conversational speaking style. She talked about herself and her credentials with enthusiasm, convincing her audience of the importance of her research. If she believed she was the expert and worthy of recognition, so would they.

Myth #7:
BRAG IS A FOUR-LETTER WORD

Brag doesn't have to be a distasteful four-letter word. Someone who is effective at self-promotion brags in a way that isn't obvious to others, and doesn't come across as too self-serving.

Learning to brag is *not* about becoming something you aren't or trying to put something over on someone. In fact, bragging as an art is just the opposite. It's about becoming more of who you are and bringing forward your best parts with authenticity, pride, and enthusiasm. It's about telling your story in a way that showcases your strengths. It's a way of building a bridge to others and to better opportunities.

Seeing it in this light, one woman pointed out that bragging is really a way of honoring our own spirits and who we really are. She noted that we do endless self-bashing along the lines of "I should be this and I shouldn't do that," or "Oh, no, I just got to the top of the publishing world because I happen, well, to be lucky." Instead, for her, bragging has become a way to revel in all the wonderful things she has accomplished.

To see bragging in this way, we have to start by wiping the slate clean and dropping our preconceived notions. As one man recently asked, "I have a boss and all he does is brag about himself. I hate it. Do I want to be one of those people? Is this what your program is all about?" Of course not. His boss is one of those people who have taken it to the extreme, who brag in a way that's annoying. But look at this man's reaction. Because of it, he doesn't brag at all, but becomes upset when recognition passes him by.

My message to all of you is simply this: You don't want to brag like "one of them," but that doesn't mean you shouldn't do it at all. Let me show you how to talk about yourself in a way that is sincere and feels comfortable. By doing so, you're going to learn how to brag *and get away with it!*

CHAPTER 2

What's So Good About You?

Wherever you go, there you are.
—BUDDHIST SAYING

- "So tell me about yourself," asks the interviewer, looking at you, then the clock.
- "What kind of sales experience do you really have?" asks a venture capitalist sizing you up.
- "Why do think you've earned a raise?" asks your boss with his eyebrow raised.
- "How have you helped me lately?" asks a demanding, high-profile client.
- "What do you do?" asks a stranger at a networking event.
- "Isn't this position really way out of your league?" asks the headhunter scanning your résumé.
- "How about introducing yourself to the group?" asks the company president your first day on the job.
- "What are you doing with yourself these days?" asks someone who has heard you've gotten axed.
- "Where did you go to school?" asks the CEO who graduated summa cum laude from Harvard.

So, what's so good about you? It's a question we are asked indirectly in our business and social interactions daily, and how we respond determines the effectiveness of our bragging campaign. Yet how many times have you walked away from a golden opportunity to strut your stuff and thought "Why did I say that?" "What was I thinking?" "If only I had said . . ."

Most of us think of the perfect thing to say about ourselves after the fact. As we later reflect on our encounters, we fantasize about how much more forthright, charming, and articulate we could have been, saying all the right things in just the right way, like characters do in movies. Then our courageous visions and thoughts slip away until the next time we are caught off-guard, when we make the same mistakes all over again. The reasons behind these lapses, as you've read thus far, are varied: entrenched bragging myths, weak interpersonal communication skills, and brag-fright. But there is also another *big* reason: We simply haven't done our homework, leaving us unprepared to field the questions thrown our way.

Effective bragging starts with *you*. It is based on having a clear sense of who you are and what you have accomplished, as well as what you are accomplishing right at this moment. It depends on your skill in communicating what makes you unique and interesting in the eyes of those you want to impress. Yet most of us remain curiously unable to articulate our stories and the diversity and extent of our skills, abilities, and attributes. We are equally unaware of how others perceive us and what exactly they like about us. We take ourselves for granted, thinking that we haven't really accomplished anything, that we're "just doing our jobs," and that the recognition we seek will naturally follow our hard work. Then reality moves in. We get overlooked for a promotion, special assignment, or pay raise. Someone else takes all the credit. We never get called back after the first round of job interviews. We get pink-slipped. We feel unappreciated and misunderstood. With life moving at such a frenetic pace, it's difficult to recall in colorful detail our successes from a month ago, much less a year or five years ago. Our accomplishments remain only as shadowy memories—that is, if we haven't forgotten them altogether. We lose track of what brought us to where we are today and how to leverage what we've got to take us where we want to go.

Despite this tendency toward amnesia, we have been accomplishing things all our lives: Since taking our first breath, we haven't stopped. We each have a history of hundreds, if not thousands, of successes that make us memorable. So how do you make certain that everyone else knows what's so good about you? You start by consciously examining your past and present life and by taking the time to dig out those golden nuggets—the ones that have substance and weight—from which to build meaningful and memorable stories and messages about *you*. This chapter will help you unearth your personal and professional history, capitalize on your strengths, learn to think fast on your feet, and convey the information you want known about yourself, genuinely and effortlessly.

On the following page you'll find "Take 12," a set of questions to help you begin to think about your history: where you have been, what you are doing now, what you have to offer, and what makes you memorable.

Take a moment right now to read these twelve questions, *but before you write down your answers,* read through the rest of this chapter. If you don't, you'll be wasting precious time and energy because first you need to understand how you'll be using your responses and turning them into catchy and immediately useable self-promotion sound bites (brag bites) and monologues (bragologues).

"Take 12" Self-Evaluation
(*Note: These questions can also be downloaded at*
www.bragbetter.com)

Don't feel that you have to answer these in order. You can start anywhere and skip around. As you move through the questions, you'll likely think of things you might have overlooked when answering earlier ones. In fact, you'll probably want to go over your responses once more after you have completed the evaluation. Remember, the more time you put into this exercise, the more specific details you provide, the easier it will be to create brag bites and bragologues that will be crystal clear and interesting to those who don't already know you well.

1. What would you and others say are five of your personality pluses?

2. What are the ten most interesting things you have done or that have happened to you?

3. What do you do for a living and how did you end up doing it?

4. What do you like/love about your current job/career?

5. How does your job/career use your skills and talents, and what projects are you working on right now that best showcase them?

6. What career successes are you most proud of having accomplished (from current position and past jobs)?

7. What new skills have you learned in the last year?

8. What obstacles have you overcome to get where you are today, both professionally and personally, and what essential lessons have you learned from some of your mistakes?

9. What training/education have you completed and what did you gain from those experiences?

10. What professional organizations are you associated with and in what ways—member, board, treasurer, or the like?

11. How do you spend your time outside of work, including hobbies, interests, sports, family, and volunteer activities?

12. In what ways are you making a difference in people's lives?

Just as you carry around your name, you carry around a history. Think of "Take 12" as an inventory of all you've done—the things you are most proud of having accomplished in your personal and professional life—not just years back, but last week as well. On a business level this might include how you landed your first job, segued from one career to another, won an important client, managed through a difficult merger, or started your business from scratch. On a personal level it might include a favorite hobby, some cause you are passionate about, a fond memory, children and loved ones, a remarkable lesson learned from a mentor, or how you climbed Mount Everest! Your combined personal and professional information acts as the foundation for your bragging campaign. It encapsulates what will most powerfully underscore your best self and what you would like other people to know about you. By answering these questions you will not only be amazed at how much you have accomplished and how interesting you are, you will also begin to *see* how the fragments of your life are actually interconnected pieces that can come together in catchy stories that will help you get the job, promotion, or recognition you are seeking.

GETTING TO KNOW YOU, GETTING TO KNOW YOU . . . AGAIN

I can hear it now, as I have so often from busy clients when faced with "Take 12": "Who has time for this?" One senior manufacturing executive complained, "I don't get into this warm and fuzzy stuff. I can't see how this exercise can help me." Upon my refusing to work with him without it, even this naysayer eventually obliged. Before I knew it, he, like those before him, returned saying, "This was eye-opening. It made me take stock—past, present, and future. For the first time, I am able to see myself more objectively. I've actually achieved a lot more than I give myself credit for."

While these twelve key questions can be completed solely by you, optimally—if you are feeling brave—you should seek input from co-workers, bosses, previous customers/clients, friends, and/or family members so that you have the broadest and most honest perspective. This is important for the simple reason that there is an amazing disconnect between who we think we are and how we actually come across to others.

In my workshops I frequently ask everyone to take a large piece of paper and list their personality pluses. When the group discusses what each person wrote down, people often disagree with someone's self-interpretation. For example, when Mr. Manufacturer, the client I dragged kicking and screaming to "Take 12," shared his pluses with the others he found that people valued his sense of humor most of all. The bottom-line perception of others: He was fun to be around. Although aware of having a playful personality, he was surprised to discover this was something co-workers and higher-ups thought made him great to work with. Ironically, he had been ever vigilant about toning down his natural tendencies in the office, thinking he would be perceived as a lightweight otherwise.

If you don't recognize the good things about yourself, you can't use them to your advantage. Your strengths become the building blocks for developing rapport with others. That doesn't mean Mr. Manufacturer becomes the office clown; rather, he reinforces a trait that is already working well in his interactions. The more feedback you can solicit from others, the easier it will be to identify your strengths and gain the most from them in future bragging opportunities.

COLORFUL DETAILS MAKE
ALL THE DIFFERENCE

Bragging comes alive with specific examples and stories. Be sure your "Take 12" answers are punctuated with colorful details, because that's what people remember. Sweeping generalities leave little or no impact, so be as explicit as possible in response to the questions.

A publicist friend of mine knows all too well the value of these details. She spends her life selling others to the media, and she frequently finds herself frustrated by her clients, noting, "A lot of supposedly savvy people just don't get it. When I ask them what they do, how they got there, the struggles, the human-interest side of the story, and try to get them to describe it in layman's terms, they automatically respond with the same boring and dry descriptions I can read on the company website. Usually it takes them a few drinks before they finally loosen up, and that's when it all comes pouring out. I get the detailed information that adds color to their campaign."

For example, when she asked the CEO of one small and highly successful Dallas software company for his story, he said he started the company at the age of twenty-three and right off the bat landed Fortune 500 companies that remain clients some twenty years hence. Scratching beneath the surface, however, she discovered: He was a technical prodigy and was hired at the age of sixteen by his best friend's father, the CEO of a major bank, to write software code for a banking program in between school hours and homework. He skipped college altogether and by age eighteen was part of the team responsible for developing the software for one of the most widely used and admired financial tracking systems in the world. That experience gave him the grounding and expertise in developing network software solutions for an area in which his company excelled. By the time my publicist friend was done grilling him, other juicy details had emerged as well. He was an advocate of children's cancer research, had equipped with global satellite tracking systems various organizations involved in saving the Amazon, and had personally funded programs that teach advanced computer-programming skills to underprivileged women.

Suddenly, Mr. Software CEO went from boring to extraordinary. In fact, his history was a goldmine of interesting information that his publicist could readily draw from to more persuasively pitch profile pieces.

YOUR BRAG BAG

After you answer the "Take 12" questions, you will have what I call your brag bag, a collection of all the information about you that's fit to mention in polite company:

your accomplishments, your passions and interests, the colorful details that describe who you are personally and professionally.

Like a candy jar filled with a variety of favorite treats, your brag bag is filled with brag bites and bragologues in all shapes and sizes, in all tastes and flavors. Brag bites are snippets of information about you, expressed in a short, pithy manner. They function as memory insurance, a way to be sure that people walk away with something compelling to remember about you. They can be dropped into conversations like gems, or woven together to create longer bragologues. Bragologues range from the thirty-second "elevator pitch" to three-minute dialogues. They are stories about yourself conveyed in a conversational style that can be stretched and blown up in a million different ways. While sometimes you'll be able to plan ahead which brag bites and bragologues to use—in performance reviews, job interviews, and formal presentations, for example—most times you'll just have to seize the opportunity on the fly. That's why you stuff your brag bag full of the brag bites and bragologues you've become completely familiar with and comfortable using in every possible combination.

Update your brag bag on a daily or weekly basis so that it is always current. Feel free to also include a private collection of anecdotes, statistics, quotations, cartoons, industry tidbits, and current events, to make your brag bites and bragologues more timely and entertaining.

Some people use a three-ring binder or a file on their computer to house their brag bag so they can readily access what they need and use it to their advantage. Your brag bag can be organized in a variety of ways. Some people compile the information chronologically. Others prefer to structure their collection by the different phases in each job or career path. Some do it by taking all their successes and prioritizing them based on short-, mid-, and long-term professional goals and objectives. Still others do it by audience and situation: "Ideal for clients," "Great speech openers and introductions," "Good facts for future job or position opportunities," "Things I need to bring forth when talking to the press," or "Must remember for future performance reviews." It's different for everyone. Experiment to find out what works best for you.

Creating Brag Bites and Bragologues

When it comes to bragging about yourself, you need to get creative in telling your story and conveying juicy nuggets about yourself. If you recite a boring list of facts, or speak in generic terms about yourself and what makes you special, you'll come off as colorless and unmemorable. And if you're one of those people who are prone to dropping brag bombs—either facts about yourself that are out of the context, scope, or spirit of the conversation or those delivered in a way that makes people yawn—you are going to come off as downright self-serving or a plain old bore. To really stick, brag bites and bragologues need to be authentic, compelling, and delivered in a conversational way. To improve their "stickiness," let me show you how others have developed brag bites and bragologues by digging deep within themselves and their experiences as they answered specific "Take 12" questions.

What would you and others say are five of your personality pluses? Roxanne wrote down that being outgoing is a personality trait she believes is a real plus and one of the first things people say about her. "So how does that help you in your work?" I ask. She responds that being outgoing means she's really interested in people. "Well, how does that translate to your job performance? Being 'interested in people' doesn't create any vision of you in my head. It sounds generic." Roxanne pauses and ponders, and then the floodgates open. She says,

> Well, as the presidential attaché at a large university, I am constantly in front of people—talking to them, putting people together, making visitors feel welcome. So it's essential that I be outgoing and friendly. The university's president, in fact, nicknamed me "den mother" the first week of work because he said that I was so good at caring for other people. My mom says I've been like this since preschool. I was always the person in charge of planning social events. So now instead of setting up slumber parties or proms, I'm in charge of arranging high-level meetings with trustees, politicians, foreign diplomats, and dignitaries, including every president from Reagan forward.

What are the ten most interesting things you have done or that have happened to you? Bev, who's forty, is a very academic type who is customer relations manager for one of my clients. Short, skinny, and somewhat shy, she has a demeanor that is so understated, she comes across as colorless and even a bit clumsy. But by telling two personal stories, she revealed a side of herself that almost knocked me over and completely changed my perception of her on the success scale. In her early twenties, she had spent three years traveling throughout Europe as the setter on a German volleyball team. Then to top that one, she taught glacier skiing in the Alps—apparently one of the most dangerous things you can do. This was completely unexpected from a gal I perceived as bookish. Once she stacked her brag bag with these two items alone, she forever changed my opinion of her.

"But . . . I'm an introvert. Talking about myself goes against my nature."

Get over it! Being an introvert won't get you noticed. Reach out beyond yourself and interact with those around you. It's the way of the world and the only way to get ahead, unless of course you're Tiger Woods or Bill Gates.

Another client who stunned me and others was Craig. He was working for a major Wall Street investment bank, managing millions of dollars for wealthy individuals. During a bragging workshop, he revealed to the group that eight years earlier he had been a "Top Gun" Navy fighter pilot who flew missions over some of the most volatile enemy territory in the world. We all practically fell off our chairs. The group agreed that this small detail was one that spoke volumes about his character, his competence, his dedication to work, not to mention his country! Craig kept responding, "It's no big deal." I suggested that he use it in a subtle way, such as, "I know what trust and responsibility are all about. As a former Navy pilot, I was entrusted every day with a twenty-five-million-dollar aircraft, carrying out missions to protect the country's interests." The very next day, Craig dropped this brag bite while pitching a new account. It turned out that the potential client was also a former Navy man, and they talked for a good half hour about their experiences. Craig was amazed when he was handed the new business on the spot.

What do you do for a living and how did you end up doing it? A physics professor at a prestigious university introduces herself as "a teacher," nothing more (boring). The technical director for research and development at a major pharmaceutical company describes himself simply as "a biochemist," nothing more (yawn). A mechanical engineer with NASA tells others he's "an engineer"(snore). All three introductions are classic brag bombs. Better brag bites would sound like these:

• "Hi, I'm Jill. I'm a physics professor. I just took on chairing the department, and now I think I have to go back and get another degree in psychology . . . or maybe even parenting."

• "Hi, I'm Ed. I'm a biochemist. I'm the kid who got a chemistry set for Christmas at age six and never stopped playing with it. Now I do research for one of the world's largest pharmaceutical companies."

• "Hi, I'm Dan. I'm one of those rocket scientists everyone always makes jokes about. I work on the space station program for NASA."

The second part of the question—how did you end up doing it?—also stumps many. It's not unusual today for people to change jobs or careers, or for individuals to move around within any organization and wear many different hats during the course of their stay. Most of us find it difficult, however, to sum up our career history in a colorful and succinct way. We tend to fall back into the laundry-list mode, a just-the-facts recitation.

A fifty-three-year-old executive named Michael, with an incredible track record, first described his career history to me like this:

I come from a broadcast background. I spent fifteen years at the major television networks, where I was producing, directing, and creating graphics for the news, entertainment, and sports divisions. I ended my stay at the network directing documentaries. After that I started my own company, where I created interactive multimedia selling materials for many multinational Fortune 500 firms. After that, I became a principal in an Internet start-up, which developed content software management for the rich-media market. I was responsible for creative services. Recently, I resigned to produce my own documentaries.

Although Michael had experienced an interesting and complex career, his description of it came off as an uninteresting recitation. We worked on linking together more specific and compelling brag bites.

I have spent all of my career in the "visual arts"—fifteen years at the major television networks directing and producing all sorts of programming from the morning shows to the World Series to sixty documentaries. I caught the Internet fever in the mid-nineties and went out on my own, producing interactive CD-ROMs for consumer-packaged-goods companies. I then got a tremendous offer to sign on for a two-year commitment with a new rich-media software developer as director of creative services, which I've just finished. Now I'm happily based at home overlooking the Berkshire Hills, working on a few new documentaries. What's even better, I no longer have a three-hour commute each day and can coach my son's Little League team.

What training/education have you completed and what did you gain from those experiences? It's really strange, but a lot of people I work with don't like to say where they went to school. One client, when asked what college he attended, wouldn't tell me, preferring instead to talk around it. When I finally called him on his caginess, he said, "Since it wasn't an Ivy League school, I don't want to tell anyone." But then, when asked where he got his graduate degree, he wouldn't tell me that either. He was afraid that because it *was* an Ivy League school (as in Harvard), he would come off sounding like a braggart. I told him he needed to stop being embarrassed on both accounts. He had to get comfortable saying where he went to under-graduate school or he would appear shifty. While I agreed that telling everyone at every opportunity that he went to Harvard would turn people off, he needed to find a subtle way to weave it into a bragologue:

> I was what you'd call a late bloomer. I wasn't a great student in high school, but fortunately what I lacked in grades I made up for in SAT scores. I went to Clemson University and got really interested in poli-tics and public affairs. After I graduated, I spent two years working in urban development in upstate New York, and then I went to the Kennedy School of Government at Harvard . . .

How do you spend your time outside of work, including hobbies, interests, sports, family, and volunteer activities? Holly, a sales manager for an insurance agency, listed her four children and their ability to get along with each other as one of her proudest achievements. Digging deep, I asked her what in that experience showcases her superior management skills on the job today. She stopped and thought. Suddenly her eyes lit up, and she said enthusiastically,

> As I was raising my four kids, I never realized how important it was going to end up being that I helped

them develop strong relationships with each other. It's turned out that their closeness is one of the things they and I value most about their relationships with each other as young adults. I'm proud they can rely on each other without having to depend on me to initiate or tend to their interactions. It's a lesson I've applied successfully to managing my group at work: I've found that the more I can help my team members foster strong connections with each other, the more independently they can function without micromanagement from me. Their autonomy frees my time up, permits them to resolve problems on their own, and ultimately leads to a more productive unit.

Bingo!

As you convert your "Take 12" responses into brag bites and bragologues, ask yourself: Am I expressing this in a way that's interesting, colorful, and showcases my competence? Am I using a beginning that hooks my listeners and an ending that leaves them satisfied or wanting to know more? Am I describing succinctly and convincingly how I segued from one career or job to another and how my experiences have culminated to make me an expert at what I do today? If you think others might react to your bragging with a resounding "So what," then start again. Remember, your bragologues are never set in stone; you will put the pieces in your brag bag together in different ways, depending on the audience and time frame.

A WEEK OF BRAGOLOGUES AND BRAG BITES

I just spent a full week, as most of us do, being exposed to endless self-promotion opportunities. I spent a total of twenty-five hours in transit in airports, airplanes, taxis, and hotel lobbies conversing mostly with strangers. I spent another thirty hours with clients on Wall Street. I spent five hours pitching new business. I spent an hour meeting with a producer from a national TV show interested in doing a communication coaching segment. I also made a forty-minute lunchtime speech to a group of lawyers. And finally, I finished up my week by attending a class reunion. Here are my brag bites and bragologues in action.

Situation: I'm on a jet bound from San Francisco to New York, and the sixty-something stranger seated next to me is reading Jim Collins's new book, *Built to Last.* Having just read and enjoyed it immensely, I lean over and engage him in a little chitchat, saying, "You are so lucky to be reading that book. I just finished it and I could read it again, it's so good."

Stranger: Oh, you must be either an executive or a consultant.

Me: Well, both, actually. I'm the executive of my own communication consulting firm. I guess that makes me a corporate mutt.

Stranger (laughing): You ought to copyright that term. What does it mean to be a communication consultant?

Me: Well, I have nothing to do with satellites or space stations. My clients are on the ground, mostly in Fortune 500 companies around the country. They're CEOs, CFOs, COOs, and all the other Os, throughout the company, who ask me to come in and coach them on everything from what I call podium skills—giving presentations to audiences of all sizes, including clients, shareholders, board members, industry and press conferences, even testifying in front of Congress—to interpersonal communication skills in areas like conflict management and leadership development. The groups I work with are as large as several hundred to a handful of people, and often just one on one. I also offer special programs about women and leadership, and teach at Wharton and at UC Berkeley's Haas MBA programs.

Stranger: Sounds interesting. How did you get into all of that?

Me: I took a wrong turn out of Hollywood and ended up on Wall Street! It all started when I was still coaching actors for television and film, broadcast anchors and reporters. I began getting panicked calls from friends on Wall Street asking for help with their client and sales presentations. They, of course, were climbing the corporate ladder and socking it away in their 401Ks. At the time I didn't think I was doing anything of great artistic importance, so I figured why not see if the coaching I was doing with all these performers would translate to the world of Brooks Brothers suits. My years in the entertainment industry included time as an actor, classical singer, director, theater and music critic, producer, and arts administrator. So I really knew the art of performing. And fortunately my hunch was right—the same skills that make performances dynamic in Hollywood can be applied with equal success to business presentation and communication. My friends and their bosses were pleased with my work, and so I started getting calls from their friends and colleagues who had noticed dramatic improvements in them. I discovered that I really liked this new way of using my skills and experience, was good at it, and could actually make money. (What a concept!) And that's how it all began.

Situation: My first meeting with a television producer who has read the *Wall Street Journal* story about my bragging workshops. She asks me to tell her a bit more about my background. Knowing that she is extremely short on time, I jump in with this:

Actually, a friend of mine says I've reinvented myself more times than anyone she knows. And I'm never quite sure if it's because I have the attention span of a gnat, or because I am really interested in so many things. I started off my career as an actor and classical singer and then became a director and producer. It may be hard to believe with my Philadelphia accent, but I actually have a licentiate in speech and drama from the Royal Academy of Music in London, signed by the Queen Mum. That all seems like a very long time ago, because for the last eight or so years I have taken all those skills I used in that performance arena and translated them into the business world, where I have been working with corporate professionals, from CEOs and CFOs and all those other Os, all the way down through the organization, in a wide cross section of industries from Wall Street to Silicon Valley, and points in between. I've coached my clients in everything from presentation skills—which most people consider getting up behind a lectern, although it's really about getting them out in front of one—to interpersonal development and leadership skills.

Situation: A lunchtime speech to a group of lawyers. I open with the following:

My father was a successful Philadelphia attorney and I was sure that I was going to follow suit—and would have, except that one summer after my freshman year in college, I was working in my dad's law firm, and the managing partner caught me doing an impression of him in the supply room. It was a really good one, too, but he didn't appreciate the nuances I brought to the performance. In fact, he rather bluntly suggested that I take my talents to the stage rather than the courtroom. So it was good-bye law school and hello to drama school in London. It's funny, today I work with a lot of attorneys and half of them tell me they wanted to be actors, except they didn't want to be the "starving actors"—definitely a smart choice! Anyway, most days my life in the entertainment business seems far away from my current incarnation as a communication consultant. And yet it was my graduate training and experience as a director and producer that give me the expertise to work with business leaders on developing executive presence, because the same skills that make performances dynamic in Hollywood can be applied with equal success to trial work and client relations.

Situation: A coaching session with my client. She asks, "How's the business?" and I reply:

You know that phrase, "Be careful what you wish for because you just might get it"? Well, I think that has happened for me. Work is fabulous. Your boss was complaining to me this morning that I don't have enough time for him anymore. In fact, he told me that I was like the mold on his shower curtain: I keep spreading through his organization. And I told him it was his own fault, because he had done such a great job turning around his communication style. Now everyone wants to follow suit. I've been very lucky and blessed. I get to do everything I love to do *and* make a living. I perform, direct, teach, write, produce, and critique really smart people, who want to improve and with whom I share a genuine connection. What could be better than that? Someone should smack me if I ever complain!

Situation: I'm courting a new client. The man I'm speaking with by phone, the CFO of a large health care organization, was referred by a friend of his, the president of a hospital in San Francisco. The first question he asks me is whether I'm a doctor. My response:

No, but I almost played one on TV! Actually, my background is in the arts, not the sciences. But because my expertise is communication, I've lectured on doctor–patient communication and personal diagnosis at the UC Berkeley School of Public Health, UC Davis, and UCSF. I have also worked with physicians to prepare them as expert witnesses for trial, press interviews, and, as I did with your friend, coached them on communication skills. For the last eight or so years, I've taken all the skills I formerly used in the performance arena and translated them into the business world, where I have been working with corporate professionals, from CEOs and CFOs and all those other Os, all the way down through the organization, in a wide cross section of industries from Wall Street to Silicon Valley, and all points in between. I've coached my clients in everything from presentation skills—which most people consider getting up behind a lectern, although it's really about getting them out in front of one—to interpersonal development and leadership skills.

Situation: My class reunion. An old friend, whom I hadn't seen since the last reunion ten years before, asks me, "Are you still working with actors and comics?" I reply, "My goodness, we haven't gotten together since I started my own firm in communication and executive coaching? I wasn't a corporate mutt just yet? Oh dear, it really has been a while. How much time do you have? This could be an all-nighter."

We chitchat some more, and then (because we really *do* have all night!) I proceed with:

So when we met last I was working in Hollywood. I began getting panicked calls from friends on Wall Street who were climbing the corporate ladder and actually making money. They were asking for help with their client and sales presentations. At the time I didn't think I was doing anything of great artistic importance, so I figured why not see if the performance coaching I was doing would translate to the world of Brooks Brothers suits. My hunch was right: The same skills actors use to make their performances dynamic are exactly what business people need in their communication. My friends were happy. Their bosses were happy. And I was happy because I really liked it, was good at it, and I could actually make money doing it. (What a concept!) I began getting calls from their friends and colleagues who had seen the improvements in them. And when a dear friend of my husband's was starting a management-consulting firm, I was asked to train her consultants in stand-up skills and marketing. I did a great job, so they referred me to their big corporate clients. I was hired to coach executives who had the Gerald Ford syndrome: They couldn't walk and talk at the same time. At the beginning this was a natural fit because of my background, but it has eventually evolved from just helping professionals give presentations to also working with them on interpersonal communication skills in areas like conflict management and leadership development. I train groups as large as several hundred to just a few people, and often one on one. I also have special programs in women and leadership, and recently have been invited to academia to torture those poor souls at Wharton and UC Berkeley's Haas MBA programs.

As you have read through my week of bragologues and brag bites, I'm sure you noticed that many key pieces in my brag bag were recycled. The situations dictated which colors and flavors I pulled out of the bag and also determined how long I took to weave "The Peggy Klaus Story." The more options you have in your brag bag, the easier it is to talk about yourself wherever you go and to make a lasting impression on whoever you encounter.

So Who Do You Want to Impress?

At a bragging workshop a woman raised her hand and said, "I've only been on the job six months, so there is no one that I really need to brag to other than my boss." I asked, "But aren't there some other people you would like to impress?" She was silent. "Look at it this way," I said. "Think about your career goals for the next six months, the next year, and the next three years." She responded that her goals included a promotion in the next nine months and eventually running the division. "So whose radar do you need to be on to ensure success?" I asked. She suddenly rattled off ten names of people within the firm and outside the firm, everyone from the CEO to professionals she had met in trade groups.

Great self-promoters are prepared to brag with anyone, anywhere, anytime. But it's also important to focus on a few key contacts, people who can make a difference in your career, and then make it a point to get in front of them. Ask yourself: Who can help me meet my goals? Of course, if you're working, you will naturally include your boss. But go beyond just him or her. Is there a colleague who has contacts? Is there an association with key members who might be important to your future? Is there a prospective customer who could become a real feather in your cap? Is there someone in your neighborhood who is highly influential in your field and worth getting to know better? Is there someone in human resources or a headhunter who could be helpful?

Don't overwhelm yourself with too many people at once. Choose five to begin with and make it your business to get to know them. First learn everything you can about their backgrounds—maybe a speech they made, where they live, whether they have kids, causes, or hobbies they are particularly passionate about. Details like these will provide a greater number of entry points for approaching them, striking up a conversation, and building a personal relationship. Approach this project with the attitude of making new friends, recognizing that the results will build over time. Remember the saying "It's not what you know, but who you know" . . . and with bragging, it's who knows you!

CHAPTER 3

The Business of Bragging In and Out of the Office

- "I got on the elevator with the chairman and didn't know what to say. It was my big chance and I blew it!"
- "I was in a meeting and the head of another division asked me my name. I've been here for nearly five years, and this guy had no clue who I was. It was embarrassing!"
- "I told them about my promotion, and there was dead silence. I'm now afraid to say another word about myself!"
- "I just worked night and day and my co-worker is stealing the spotlight!"
- "I always take lunch at my desk. Who has time for idle chat?"
- "All I need is to deliver the numbers. They speak for themselves!"
- "Put me in front of five thousand people, but please don't make me go to one of those corporate cocktail events!"

- "I've sat in on way too many business pitches where the presenters are focused entirely on themselves and their accomplishments."
- "I thought that my co-workers would think I was kissing up! So I never approached the director at the dinner."

Getting the credit and recognition you want takes work. And I am not talking about slaving away at your desk night after night, assuming that the rest of the world will put two and two together. Or about waiting for the teacher to stamp a gold star on your book report so that you can advance to the head of the class. I mean taking it *solely* upon yourself to show the world on a daily basis—in a gracious and genuine manner—who you are and what you have done, so you gain the recognition and credit that you deserve and that you need to succeed. Whether it's office talk, elevator talk, meeting talk, lunch talk, dinner talk, watercooler talk, hallway talk, event talk, networking talk, or even rest room talk, your self-promotion campaign starts and is sustained by *you*. Bragging is all about getting your name out front and center, and your accomplishments circulated, recirculated, freshened and refreshened, time and time again—all in a way that doesn't come across as disingenuous or too "Me! Me! Me!"

ALWAYS BE ARMED AND READY

"I got on the elevator with the chairman and didn't know what to say. It was my big chance and I blew it!"

It's the first month on the job for Alex, the assistant to the chief information officer. He's at a trade show to check out the competition. It's his last day at the event and he has loads of juicy insights to share with his new boss that are sure to impress him. In between sessions, Alex gets on the elevator with a stranger and it stops just before reaching the conference floor. The chairman of his company gets on. Whoa! Alex didn't expect him to be there. No one had told him. (Alex had thought he was fly-fishing in Alaska.) This is his moment—but he freezes. Completely blindsided, he's not sure what to say. So he doesn't say anything. Then the absolute worst thing happens. Mr. Chairman turns to him and says, "I see from your badge we work for the same company. I'm Bob Mayers." Alex replies, "Yes, I know who you are. I was too embarrassed to say hello." (Did those words really come out of his mouth? Yes, and after they did, he beat himself up for two days straight.)

What he could have said, warmheartedly, with a sincere smile and a handshake, was, "Hi, Mr. Mayers. I'm Alex Scott. I just joined the company a month ago. I'm the CIO's new assistant and very excited to be here." Stepping off the elevator with Mr. Chairman as he entered the lobby, he could have whispered, "It's been great being here. I've spent the last three days sizing up our competition from every angle. I'd love to make an appointment with you sometime next week to tell you what I've learned."

Now, what was so hard about that?

Step one of your bragging campaign is quite simple. Every day remind yourself of four things: your name, your title, your responsibilities, and the positive things you are accomplishing *right now* for your organization. Have them on the tip of your tongue, raring to go. Leave things to chance and you'll find yourself rambling, stumbling, and missing out when opportunities come calling on the fly. Whether it's on the elevator, at the watercooler, around the coffeepot, on an airplane, or waiting for a taxi, you need to have your brag bag with you at all times. "Shoulda, woulda, coulda" isn't going to get you to where you want to go. Be ready to seize the chance to self-promote at a moment's notice.

DON'T ASSUME ANYTHING

"I was in a meeting and the head of another division asked me my name. I've been here for nearly five years, and this guy had no clue who I was. It was embarrassing!"

We all need to become like Mr. Chairman in the elevator, who so graciously extended himself. Yet many people shy away from introducing themselves, especially to higher-ups. And when they do work up the courage, they mumble their names at an inaudible level, as if they are embarrassed to get any attention. At larger organizations in particular, people often skip this basic courtesy entirely. They assume that everyone will magically know who they are and what they do, or that those who need to know them will beat a path to their door. Skillful self-promoters know better.

Marilyn, a senior broker in the retail division of a major financial institution, learned the hard way. She has been with the company for more than five years, and is considered a star player in her division. For the past year she has been eyeing possible openings in private banking, and doing her best to help out brokers in that division when they call asking for favors in a crunch. At a meeting she attended recently, where several managers from each of the company's core divisions met, her boss casually mentioned, "Marilyn will take care of those numbers." The private-banking head asked, "Who's Marilyn?"

"I was shocked," said Marilyn. "My face actually flushed. I became beet red. There was no way I could hide my embarrassment." She added, "Here I had been going out of my way for brokers in that division for twelve months, but somehow my name hadn't trickled up to their senior management." After that, Marilyn kicked her self-promotion campaign into high gear. She not only completed the requested report in record time, but also took the opportunity to personally deliver it to Mr. Private-Banking Head. When he thanked her for the quick turn-around, she took the opportunity to tell him how interested she was in shifting to his division. He invited her back for a talk and was surprised to find out how much she already knew about the division, having participated, however indirectly, in some of the bigger projects. Within six months she was offered the transfer she had hoped for, reporting directly to Mr. Private-Banking Head.

For the rest of your career, when you are in a meeting, look around the room and, size permitting, make it a point to personally introduce yourself to every single person in the room. When doing so, imagine you are introducing a very good friend and not yourself. It makes it much easier. Just do it. Say your name, mention what you do with a smile and upbeat energy, and then let the bragging begin.

TIMING AND DELIVERY ARE EVERYTHING

"I told them about my promotion, and there was dead silence. I'm now afraid to say another word about myself!"

You'll know your bragging has bombed when your listeners suck in what you've said and they hardly say a word in response. You either suddenly feel like you would rather be as tiny as that crumb on the floor, or you're so self-absorbed that the silence goes right over your head as you keep blabbing away, sinking yourself deeper and deeper. A brag bomb is often the result of bad timing, a bad read on your audience, or both.

Let's take Anne. She has been putting in long hours with her co-workers for more than two years. The company is fiscally strapped, and there has been a freeze on salary increases for nearly a year. They've all been reporting to a slave-driver of a boss. While her co-workers have whined, she's been angling for a better position in a new department. Anne learns that her efforts have been so successful, she has been asked not only to join the new department, but to run it as well. At a weekly project status meeting with her co-workers, she bursts into the room, interrupting the discussion, and announces: "You won't believe what just happened. I got the promotion! I am going to be heading the new customer service department with thirty people reporting to me. This is big, my friends."

Here it comes: that deafening silence. What went
wrong? First, she rudely interrupted a meeting. Second,
she forgot to take the emotional temperature of her audience. How can you expect co-workers who are down-
trodden by hard work and little pay to greet such news
with applause? The way she delivered her message was
better suited to those outside her immediate ring.

Anne's interests would have been better served if she
had communicated the news in such a way that it had a
positive value for those on the receiving end. She also
could have waited to make the disclosure at the end of the
meeting. Then her bragologue might have sounded like
this:

> I got word today that I am going to be heading the
> new customer service department. It's a good oppor-
> tunity and step up for me, something that I've wanted
> for a long time. Although I'm sorry to say I won't be
> working with you directly, I am going to be looking
> to you guys when it's time for me to expand or re-
> place new people in my area. I have a lot of respect
> for each of you and I really appreciate how hard
> you've worked.

The art of tooting your own horn is knowing when and
how to toot. It's always keeping your sensitivity antenna
raised. For example, a funeral is hardly the appropriate
time to launch into a bragologue. Walking into your boss'
office when he or she is immersed in a crisis makes equally
poor bragging sense. And don't make the fatal mistake of
lobbing your brag bites and bragologues into conversations

where they don't belong. If you're intent on making a few self-promo points, work the conversation so that you introduce them naturally. If you can't do that, wait for a better opportunity. Even if you get the context right and the style right, recognize that no matter what you say or how you say it, some people are simply not going to be happy for you. Period. Don't let that stop you. Just walk around them and move on.

STEP INTO THE SPOTLIGHT

"I just worked night and day and my co-worker is stealing the credit!"

There's nothing worse than credit theft on the job. Yet when co-workers claim credit for the ideas of others or steal the spotlight, most people retreat or bite their tongues. If they do speak up, they're afraid they will come off as whiners or whistle-blowers. And isn't it better anyhow to stay invisible and demonstrate self-sufficiency, the belief being "The less I bother my boss, the better and stronger I look"?

This mentality has been thirty-four-year-old Tom's modus operandi. But the arrival of Julie, who has been assigned to work alongside him in his department, has changed all that. "She's her own one-woman PR machine. We're supposed to be a team, but every second she can she gets out there with this 'I'm doing everything' circus act. In fact, when she sees that the boss is on the phone, Julie will stand there waiting for her to hang up. She is so over the top, I don't know how to rein her in," he says.

"But . . . if you're at the top of your game, why do you need to self-promote?"

Because no matter how high you go, you always need to prove yourself. The higher you climb, the more that's expected of you. So you'd better speak up for yourself. Plus, as they say in show business, you're only as good as your last film.

Tom's strategy for foiling this credit robbery is all wrong. Instead of reining Julie in, he should be planning his own attack, figuring out ways to be seen and heard while taking ownership of his own ideas. A revised bragging plan for Tom is amazingly simple and effective. It begins with him freshening up his bragologue by making a list of everything he has accomplished in the last few months and is planning to work on soon. Once a week he sends this list to his boss, then follows up with a phone call to discuss it. Before each meeting that she is going to attend with him, he shoots off an e-mail to her outlining his ideas. After the meeting he follows up with another note proposing the next steps. He copies everyone in attendance, including Julie. At client luncheons Tom now gets up and introduces himself, talking about his long history in the department. He religiously meets his boss once a month for lunch. And then to really top it off, he even compliments Julie to her face in the boss' presence for her hard work. This simple gesture raises Tom up a notch by making him appear gracious, knowledgeable, and filled with true team spirit—all the qualities of an up-and-coming player.

GATHER AROUND THE WATERCOOLER

"I always take lunch at my desk. Who has time for idle chat?"

The corporate canteen for lunch, the watercooler, the coffeepot, or vending machines for impromptu gatherings are key bases in your bragging operations. Although generally taken for granted, these spots provide nearly constant opportunities to gain a stronger personal footing with people you may want to impress.

I can hear it now. Business is business and break time is *my* time. One of my clients, Lucille, used to be a perfect example of this attitude. She always ate lunch at her desk. Frustrated with her lack of progress on the career front, I suggested she change her ways and use lunchtime as an opportunity to casually get to know others. She went along reluctantly at first, coming back to me five lunches later saying, "I've been chatting it up, and I've even met a few interesting people, but where has it really gotten me?" I sent her back, insisting that she keep to her promise to try it for two months. A few weeks later, I got an enthusiastic call from Lucille, saying, "Well, how do you like that? Who would have ever believed it, but a woman I spoke to at lunch about my BA in women's studies mentioned to the human resources director that she should check me out to run the company's new diversity effort.

The director just called and I'm meeting her next week."
It's easier to accomplish the big things in our bragging
campaigns when we wake up to the littlest opportunities
that were in front of us all along.

DON'T LET YOUR NUMBERS DO ALL THE TALKING

*"All I need is to deliver the numbers. They speak for them-
selves!"*

How many times have you sat in a weekly status meeting and heard people moan and groan about the issues
they are facing in trying to achieve their goals and objectives? In your next meeting, try something completely different. Share your successes and the tough spots you've
turned golden. Do it once, and I can guarantee that your
bragging campaign will hit high gear and immediately
begin to earn dividends that will pay out over time.

"What's the point, Peggy?" asks Gwen, a sales rep in the
pharmaceutical industry. "My bosses see my numbers, and
that's all they want to hear about—that I've met the goals."
I respond, "People like to learn from others how they have
overcome obstacles. It's one of the best bragging tools in
your arsenal." At my urging, Gwen kept a running log
every day for the next week. She looked beyond the numbers, and started to write down in detail how she managed
to win accounts. At her next meeting, recalling one of her
recent victories, she explained to the group how she had
worked on one big client for nearly two years:

He had been on the fence for so long. Many times I was ready to give up, but every month I got in a call, just to banter and check on what he was up to and how business was going. When I saw a news clip or a research report that I thought would be of interest, I sent it his way. Suddenly last week, out of the blue, I got a call from him. He had just received the funding he needed, and bingo, I was the first person he contacted. To everyone here, who feels frustrated, remember to keep plugging away. Persistence pays off.

For the next six months, Gwen kept to this positive tone in her weekly status meetings. Before she knew it, her bosses were thinking of her as a "beyond the numbers" kind of gal. In fact, the way she inspired the group had the markings of a good manager and leader. And when one of her bosses was promoted, he recommended that she fill his shoes.

BREAK THE ICE

"Put me in front of five thousand people, but please don't make me go to one of those corporate cocktail events!"

Ask ten people what they dread most in business, even more than public speaking, and high on their list will be attending office social affairs or networking events where they know few of the other guests. One of my clients, an Alec Baldwin look-alike, works for a major oil and gas company and has just returned from a two-year assignment in Russia overseeing a new operation. He's funny

and charming—a man of many words—until he walks
into a crowded room, and then suddenly all the life is
sucked out of him. He becomes, in a word, speechless. The
feelings he describes are similar to what I've heard from
many other clients: "Dread. I feel like a lone animal in the
wilderness. I can't think of anything to say. It's hard
enough for me to even talk to people I know, and now
you're telling me I have to brag to perfect strangers?"

But social phobia can be overcome. As I told Mr. Oil
and Gas, set an objective that's not too daunting. Make a
promise with yourself that you will make contact with
three people. There are all sorts of easy tricks you can use
to break the ice. One is to acknowledge the elephant in the
room—that is, to announce to the person next to you in
the buffet line that you know absolutely no one and that
it's at these times you think to yourself "Why did I ever
decide to leave home?" By being candid and upfront, you
are taking the charge out of the uncomfortable situation,
creating a very real and honest ground on which to extend
the conversation. Another way is to go over and say to
someone, "You look about as unfamiliar with this as I am."
On an elevator filled with other people attending the same
event, try striking up a conversation with one of them, so
when you enter the event you don't feel so alone. Besides,
by the time you get into the room you will probably still
be talking and will likely end up sitting with the person
and being introduced to his contacts.

After you get beyond breaking the ice, the opportunities for promoting yourself will flow if you're prepared. For
Mr. Oil and Gas, we worked on several brag bites, his favorite being "I would gladly take the tundra any day over

wearing a black tie." It all comes back to a simple premise: The more people who know who you are and what you do the better, because you never know where opportunity is going to come from. To be a successful self-promoter you need to adopt schmoozing and cruising as a way of business, a way of surviving, and a way of getting ahead. Think of it as a career maker or breaker.

"But . . . do I really need to brag 24/7?"

Like the Scouts, be prepared . . . to toot at any time. That doesn't mean, however, that you do it *all* the time or that you do it at inappropriate times or places. You do it when it feels comfortable. And learning how to make it feel more comfortable is what this book is all about.

MAKE IT MEANINGFUL

"I've sat in on way too many business pitches where the presenters are focused entirely on themselves and their accomplishments."

Bryan, a fifty-something financial consultant based in New York City, is working on a new business pitch for the director of a family foundation in the Boston community. I asked Bryan to let me hear how he was going to introduce himself and his team members. After he finished, I wished I hadn't asked. What I got was a three-minute, nonstop chronological recap of where and with whom on Wall Street he had worked since college. After Bryan brought me up to his present job, he then tortured me with another two minutes devoted to the other members of his pitch team. It had to rank as one of the top-ten most boring introductions I had ever heard.

I asked Bryan how what he just said related to the potential client. In other words, why should this person care? "Well, obviously it shows that I've been in the business a long time and worked with a lot of good firms and people, and that I have the experience," he replied.

While all that was true, I gently broke the news that the excellent recall of his career didn't speak to who he was, how he collaborated with clients, and how his past successes directly related to the prospect's situation. And worse than all of that, he left out the most important fact. The prospect wanted a financial adviser with strong ties to the Boston community, but Bryan forgot to mention that he was a native of the area, that he had attended both graduate and undergraduate school in Boston, and that his ninety-three-year-old mother, as well as all his relatives, lived within a fifteen-mile radius of the foundation's office!

"Geez, how could I have overlooked something so simple?" Bryan asked with his head hung low. He took a deep breath, straightened up, smiled, and started again:

Hello, everyone. I want to thank you for having us up here today. My ninety-three-year-old mother, who still lives in my childhood home in Waltham, says thank you. My coming here on business means that she now gets to have her son take her to her favorite restaurant. Actually, many of us are natives of the area. I went to Brandeis and got an MBA from Tufts. Henry grew up in Wooster, crossed the state line to go to Brown for a few years, and he heads up our office here. Both of us have had a lot of experience working with private family foundations of varying sizes. We have helped families who are in the beginning stages—as yours is—in determining the focus, setting up the organization, hiring the personnel and acting as consultant once the foundation is up and running. This is all in addition to our financial responsibilities of . . .

It's amazing to me how often people dash off to new-business presentations without spending the time to really think through how what they are going to say is of benefit to the prospective clients and customers. Your bragging campaign will completely flop if you don't serve up yourself and your credentials in ways that have specific value and meaning for your audience. If something in your history has no benefit, then drop it and rework your bragologue to focus on the most compelling points of your background and successes.

THROW KISSES

"I thought that my co-workers would think I was kissing up! So I never approached the director at the dinner."

I always thought peer pressure went out the window once adulthood set in, but amazingly it is alive and thriving on the playgrounds of corporate America. A client named Denzell, a twenty-six-year-old insurance executive in the initial stages of his bragging campaign, had been angling for months to meet up with someone powerful at his firm whom he had targeted as absolutely imperative to get to know. Mr. Higher-Up was on the road nearly nonstop, and it had been difficult for Denzell to connect with him.

A perfect opportunity, however, presented itself at the company's Christmas party. Mr. Higher-Up was not only there, but was seated alone at his table for a large part of the evening. You would think that Denzell would have jumped all over this chance, but his mission got scuttled for the silliest of reasons: He didn't want to appear to his co-workers like he was kissing up. It was better not to run the risk of potentially exposing himself to their jealousy and judgments, and quite possibly ridicule and back-stabbing. He might blow his image as a team player. It was much safer to be discreet, stay with his pack, and roam the room in obscurity. There would always be other less public opportunities.

If you want to get ahead, I have one response to the kissing-up dilemma that Denzell and so many of my other clients grapple with: *Get over it.* The game of getting ahead is the game of being secure and confident in blazing your own trail, and getting in front of the people you need to impress. It's fine to have co-workers whom you enjoy and respect and to behave as a team player, but what isn't so fine is succumbing to a herd mentality—to your own detriment, no less. People would rather be approached at a time that they have committed for open-ended mingling and conversing than when they are busy and involved in other things. The very fact they are at a public event is an invitation for you to engage them. And here is another secret: A lot of very senior executives whom I've coached have remarked that they often find themselves seated alone at corporate functions because so many people are afraid to approach them. The CEO lonely for some companionship? You bet.

CHAPTER 4

———————◎———————

Techno-Brag:
Tooting in the 21st Century

- "I never see my boss anymore."
- "I don't see how bragging will warm up my cold calls."
- "His bragging was a complete turnoff over the phone, but in person it worked."
- "I'm nervous about my virtual presentation to a customer whom I've never met."
- "I'm afraid my lack of visibility has hurt me since I've been telecommuting."
- "The only time I hear from him is when he wants to toot his own horn."
- "His e-mail has come back to haunt him."

When I talk to my clients about bragging over the wires, they complain, "It's too impersonal." But when I talk to my clients about bragging in person, it elicits the opposite response: "It's too personal."

So there you are: You can't win for losing! But let's face it, more and more workplace communication today is faceless, and if you ignore this critical detail in your bragging campaign, you're most likely to come up short. Learning how to take advantage of technology—to cast yourself in the best light and deliver your message with impact—is an essential skill when you're promoting yourself in an e-mail, selling yourself on a voice mail, or tooting your own horn into the telephone receiver.

Techno-bragging can be used to keep people you want to impress up to speed on your progress and successes in an instant, whether you're traveling, based thousands of miles from headquarters, have customers and co-workers scattered around the globe, or even when you're in the office and can't catch your boss or the person in the cubicle next to you!

It can be used to open doors that were once closed, letting you make personal contact with professionals whose opinions count. A rather timid junior client of mine was so excited about a speech given by the CEO of his corporation, one of the largest packaged-goods companies in the world, that he boldly sent off an e-mail telling her how her words of advice helped him land a new client. A few days later he got a call and was invited up to the CEO's office to meet her.

Effective techno-bragging can keep you in the front of every key person's mind for all sorts of career opportunities. One client of mine targeted the company human resources director, whom he first met while interviewing for his job, as someone whose radar screen he wanted to stay on. Even though three thousand miles separated them, he communicated with her casually every few months by dropping her an e-mail and occasionally calling to discuss

how things were going for her, asking what she was working on. Eighteen months later, and before it was posted on
the company's intranet, he got a call from her about a
great opportunity within the organization that was right
up his alley. He was able to get a jump on angling for the
position, calling the team manager and introducing himself. Two months later, he landed the job.

Who can ignore the power of today's technology? The
Internet, World Wide Web, and intranets all place insight-
ful information at our fingertips that can help us look
smarter in our bragging campaigns. There's nothing more
impressive or noteworthy than someone who has taken the
time to find out everything about your background, your
company, or your business. Armed with up-to-date information, effective self-promoters position themselves more
strategically while at job interviews, pitching new business,
working with clients and customers, and even maneuvering within their own companies.

Techno-bragging, however, is significantly different
from face-to-face self-promotion, where facial expressions,
tone of voice, and body language all help to persuasively
sell ourselves. In the absence of visual cues, what we say
and how we say it—whether written in e-mail, stated on
a voice mail, or expressed over a telephone—becomes crit-
ically important. To stay visible and make a good impression, become a master of technology so that your unique
personality still comes across in your bragging.

LEARN HOW TO REPLACE FACE TIME

"I never see my boss anymore."

Not long ago all we had to do in order to strut our stuff was to get to the office. Because everyone generally worked on-site, there were more opportunities for face-to-face interaction. We could go from desk to desk, meeting to meeting, and hobnob in the hallway or around the coffeepot. Significant others like our bosses could actually see how hard we were working. But that scenario is changing. Thanks to the fax, Internet, mobile phone, and laptop computer, your boss—or really anyone, for that matter—is more frequently working from everywhere but the office!

George, a financial analyst, was feeling neglected by Liz, his boss of two years. Until about six months ago, the two had sat side by side, where he was able to give her daily detailed updates about his efforts, and she could literally see how hard he was working. Then the investment bank underwent a major merger. Liz's region was redefined, her direct reports expanding from five people to fifteen, and from seventy-five employees at one site to nearly two hundred in three offices along the northeastern seaboard.

Since the merger George has become increasingly frustrated with his attempts to get in front of his boss for some quality time. Lately Liz is rarely in the office, her secretary screens and replies to all e-mails, and the only way to get an immediate response from her is via voice mail. George, unfortunately, feels uncomfortable constantly leaving voice mails for routine matters and even more uneasy leaving ones where he might come off as tooting his own horn. It's one thing to subtly promote himself to his boss in face-to-face encounters within the context of a conversation, it's an entirely different matter to dial Liz's extension and shout into the voice mail void, "Oh, by the way, since you weren't here and missed seeing it, I did a bang-up job today!"

Preferring the traditional in-person approach, George has chosen to wait for the one day each week when his boss is scheduled to be in the office. So he waits and waits. When Liz finally shows up, she might as well as have a "Do not disturb" sign hanging on her door. Her calendar is booked with back-to-back meetings. Every spare moment she seems engulfed in preparing for the next appointment. Increasingly desperate, George even resorted at one point to monitoring her powder room visits. But on his first approach, she hurried by with a wave and a smile before he could get a single word out of his mouth. Well, I'll bet you can guess the rest of this story. The weeks stretched out and before long, George was pretty much off Liz's radar screen completely while plenty of others seemed to be on it.

When George asked me for a way around his problem, I told him his days of avoiding voice mail, Liz's technology of choice, had to come to an immediate end. Since his boss seemed to be checking her voice mail on the run, I reminded him to keep his messages short and pithy; the last thing she wanted was to listen to a long, drawn-out tale. I advised him to check in every day, keeping her current on the progress he was making with his most important projects. I reminded him to keep his bragologues conversational, interesting, and enthusiastic. We practiced with a project he just completed: "Good news, Liz. I just wrapped up getting Joe Littlefield's portfolio in order. We still need to iron out a few kinks on the mutual funds side, but he's very pleased with my efforts. I consider those challenges secondary and expect to have all issues worked out by the end of the week. Joe and I are meeting this Wednesday."

The following day, Liz responded immediately. "I loved hearing about your work with Joe. Thanks for letting me know what you're up to. Call me after your meeting with him to give me an update." George took my suggestion and called her daily for three weeks, then tapered off to every other day, unless there was something pressing. Next time Liz was in the office she said, "Stop by later this afternoon. I have another project that I could use your help on."

In today's wired world, you need to master technology and become a virtual extrovert. When contact is infrequent, people tend to think the worst about you, or even worse, think nothing about you at all. Be proactive in your virtual communication so that your presence is felt daily. Keep it constant and keep it coming.

DEVELOP A STORY

"I don't see how bragging will warm up my cold calls."

Do you find yourself leaving messages with customers but never getting a return call? Today's technology offers more choices than ever for promoting ourselves, but for many, getting noticed has never been tougher. While it may seem like technology has made selling yourself easier, the reality is that more than ever, voice mail messages go unreturned and e-mails get deleted. If you are leaving predictable and canned messages, you may have only yourself to blame.

Selling Girl Scout cookies had been Gina's highest level of experience in fundraising until she became responsible for raising a million dollars for a public television series she was producing. After being sent to voice mail 99.9 percent of the time when phoning potential sponsors, she quickly became frustrated at the very start of her campaign. Other than saying her name, the halfhearted messages she left went something like this: "Hi. I'm calling to, um, ask if you might be interested in, um, becoming an underwriter for an exciting new public television series that requires a million-dollar budget. If you are interested, please call me for more information. Thank you."

It didn't surprise me that nobody, but nobody, ever got back to her. My first question to Gina was, "Tell me why anyone would call you back?" And she said, "Oh Peggy, this project is going to be the most amazing one I have ever worked on! We'll be taping on location in six countries, including China. This will be my sixth series. The last one not only won several prestigious awards, but also set a distribution record for being picked up by more stations, and seen by more viewers, than any other program of its kind. I've carefully targeted companies with incredible potential to benefit from being associated with this project, given their products." I put my head on the desk and started to laugh. There was her bragologue! With a message like that, the wires should be burning up with callbacks.

So we started again, this time using some of the above bragologue and adding Gina's own impressive credentials as a producer. She dropped in the brag bite about the ways each company could benefit from becoming a sponsor. And she stopped mentioning the daunting amount of the total budget. She delivered her bragologue with the same enthusiasm in her voice as when she told me about the project. Here is one she used when pitching the marketing director for a global electronics manufacturer, which landed her an immediate callback. After stating her name and company, she said:

> I'm a television producer working on an educational documentary series on how global trade is raising the standard of living for people in Asia. This will be my sixth series—the last one reached all-time rating highs and set distribution records. I know that you have a very strong footing in Asia, and I would love the opportunity to describe how you could benefit from being associated with our program, which will attract millions of viewers. I look forward to hearing from you soon so that we can discuss the many opportunities we offer our sponsors. Once again, my name and number are . . .

It's important to remember that a voice mail message is often your first shot at making a memorable impression. Just as when you prepare for an in-person presentation, take the time to script what you are going to say. Consider the points you want to make, working them into pithy and personalized thirty-second bragologues that you can string together in different ways to come across as conversational, not canned. Speak slowly and enunciate clearly. Smile as you dial so your voice comes across with vitality and warmth.

PUT YOUR BEST SELF ON THE LINE

"His bragging in person was a complete turnoff over the phone, but in person it worked."

Often when we brag long-distance, the signals we send out can easily appear less than genuine or likeable, especially in an initial encounter. Without seeing and experiencing the person on the other end, our first impressions of someone can be distorted, as the following story illustrates.

Eric and Sally had scheduled a meeting with Harry, head of computer science at a prominent university, to see a demo of the software product he had developed and that their company was considering adding to its line. Eric was meeting Harry face to face, with Sally conferenced in by phone.

When Harry arrived a few minutes late, he entered the room with a burst of energy, literally. He was in athletic gear and all sweaty, having just finished his five-mile morning run. Eric was taken aback. Harry most definitely wasn't the bow-tie, understated academic type. He smiled at Eric and extended a warm hello while looking him straight in the eye and asking him to excuse his appearance. Harry quickly grabbed a fresh T-shirt from his file cabinet and told Eric he would be right back. While he was changing, Eric conferenced Sally on the speakerphone. When Harry returned, he offered Eric a cup of coffee. Eric liked him immediately. Although somewhat eccentric, Harry was definitely charming.

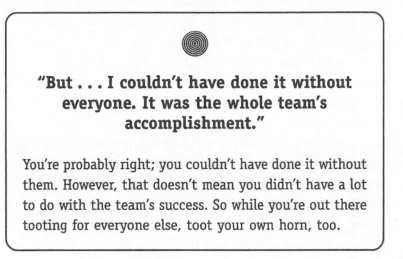

"But . . . I couldn't have done it without everyone. It was the whole team's accomplishment."

You're probably right; you couldn't have done it without them. However, that doesn't mean you didn't have a lot to do with the team's success. So while you're out there tooting for everyone else, toot your own horn, too.

Eric introduced Sally over the speakerphone, but Harry barely acknowledged her and launched into his presentation. "Let me tell you a little bit about myself," he said, and then went into a five-minute monologue about his history and successes. Although Harry's self-introduction sounded like a pompous dissertation to Sally, Eric found it amusing and entertaining. As Harry spoke he smiled, made eye contact, and seemed genuinely excited about his work, pointing to the various devices on his desk that he had invented and the numerous awards lining his office walls. Eric was impressed. Sally was completely turned off.

Why did Harry bomb so badly with Sally in his bragging campaign?

Well, as Elizabeth Barrett Browning said, let me count the ways! Overall, he never built a bridge to Sally. First, he barely interacted with her, relegating her to a secondary, almost invisible status. In fact, at one point he knocked the speakerphone off his desk and kept going as if nothing had happened. Second, although Harry engaged in a little bit of small talk with Eric when they first met, he made no attempt to break the ice with Sally. When he offered Eric coffee, he could have said, "Sally, we have a fresh pot of coffee; I wish I could offer some to you!" Third, Harry didn't modify his communication so that Sally could get a clearer picture of what he was talking about. For example, when he picked up one of his inventions he should have said something like, "Sally, I'm showing Eric my invention, the first computer input device, which looks just like a ball of wires with a pointer on it." He never described it because he was playing to Eric who could see it, and not to Sally who could not. Instead, all Sally heard was a boring recitation of his inventions, one after another. Without visual cues, listening to Harry over the telephone for ten minutes felt like an eternity.

Today people come together in all sorts of ways. A meeting could easily be a mix of people who are actually there and people who aren't. In your techno-bragging efforts, find ways to connect with everyone and to compensate for the lack of visual cues for those connected remotely. Otherwise, your bragging is bound to offend.

REACH OUT

"I'm nervous about my virtual presentation to a customer whom I've never met."

Many of us, particularly at the junior level in an organization, never meet clients and customers. Twenty-three-year-old Janine was one of them. An assistant to the managing director of a major sales region, she was just getting started on Wall Street when she was asked to quickly pull together a sales orientation for a new customer and to present it via computer. She wanted to make the customer feel secure that she knew what she was doing, but at the same time felt unsteady meeting him for the first time in a long-distance presentation, with three of her more experienced associates in other parts of the country listening in. She felt equally unsettled about doing a bragologue in front of the group, especially since they all knew she was green. Janine was so nervous about the presentation that she was losing sleep over it. To overcome her paralyzing reluctance, I advised her to conduct a little background research on the customer. Then she should pick up the phone and call him, introduce herself, explain she was preparing this orientation on his behalf, and ask if there were any particular areas he would like her to cover in more depth than others. Janine looked at me with a sigh of relief, and said, "Of course!" She later called him and left this voice mail:

Bill, this is Janine with Bluestar. I've worked with Marta for two years, and as you know she asked me prepare a presentation for next Thursday as an orientation to the firm. I want to make it as meaningful as possible for you, so I've spent several days checking out your portfolio and I noticed that you're heavily invested in a few key markets. As it turns out, my expertise is in those areas! Of course I will cover them in the orientation, but I'd like to talk to you before Thursday about any other interests you might have, so I can make sure that experts in those fields are present at our meeting. And by the way, I noticed you and I share something else in common: I'm also from Chicago, born and raised there. Give me a call back at your convenience. My number is . . .

How long do you think it took for this new client to return Janine's call? Within an hour she'd heard back from him and they spent a good thirty minutes talking about their common backgrounds and the areas of interest he wanted included in the presentation. The day she gave her virtual presentation, the client paid the ultimate compliment before she even got started. He told the group how much he appreciated Janine's call, and her Midwestern style of welcoming him on board. Janine's boss immediately took note of her budding customer-relations skills.

Last month when Janine was in California she gave me a call. We hadn't spoken in ages. She had moved up the corporate ladder a few rungs and told me that her biggest client was none other than the one she had called a few years back at my urging. She said it was one of the best pieces of advice she had ever received. From then on, she had never gone cold into any presentation or pitch without first checking her brag bag, doing a little investigating, and then calling ahead to have a personal one-on-one chat with the prospective client. It was no wonder to me that in addition to breaking the ice, she was breaking all-time sales records for her region.

GET A PLAN IN PLACE

"I'm afraid my lack of visibility has hurt me since I've been telecommuting."

"I'm miserable. I just found out I was overlooked again for a gem assignment. And guess who beat me out? Another telecommuter with half my experience!" said Betsy, an assistant art director who at thirty-five has been working for a large multinational advertising agency for more than a decade. A year before, with the birth of her first child, she had taken maternity leave and then, like so many women, decided to avoid the long commute and stay closer to home. She asked her boss for a full-time telecommuting arrangement. Given her excellent track record, the company was eager to keep her on.

For the last year the arrangement had worked well, but Betsy had a nagging feeling that despite her good work, her professional star was falling. More and more she was being handed second-tier assignments, and now she had just been passed over for a big account that was right up her alley. When she called her boss and asked point-blank why she had been overlooked, he said that the other telecommuter had been doggedly pursuing this assignment for a month, had done some fabulous work with another client, and had spent a day in the office introducing herself to all the members of the new account team. Quite frankly, he hadn't even thought about giving it to Betsy, because she seemed to have her hands full. Her competition had beaten her at the bragging game!

Betsy and I sat down and spent a good two hours completely dissecting her self-promotion efforts since she began telecommuting. It was immediately clear from the get-go that she had no plan in place. Communication with her boss was typically by e-mail, and sometimes by phone, "as needed," and usually focused on putting out fires. There was no designated day or time for regular dialogue. Since she started working from home, she had narrowed her interaction and communication to only those working on the account: her boss, the account director, the copywriter, and, of course, the client. She had lost contact with co-workers and many of the higher-ups in other departments because she felt strange calling them or e-mailing them just to say hello. She rarely traveled to the home office because most meetings, which she attended about once a month, were held at the client's location. In the last year she had visited the office on three occasions, once to show off her new son, and the other times to participate in all-day strategy sessions that afforded her little chance to do anything but get in and out. She also missed all sorts of schmoozing opportunities: the company's holiday party, its annual summer barbecue, and two walk-a-thons to raise money for medical research. She had definitely taken herself out of the loop. By the time Betsy was finished explaining all of this to me, it was crystal clear why she was suffering from the "out of sight, out of mind" syndrome.

So we put together a thoughtful and deliberate plan to raise her profile:

1. Arrange a designated time each week for a talk with her boss, during which she would underscore how well she was performing. Regularly send e-mail updates to him about her accomplishments and any positive client feedback.
2. Check in with colleagues by phone and e-mail a few times a week not only to let them know what she's up to, but also to find out what's going on in the office.
3. Pick out five people in the firm who she needs to establish her visibility with. Create a techno-bragging trail with them, and schedule monthly trips to the city to meet with them and her boss for lunch.
4. Make it a priority to attend corporate functions and to get involved in helping organize an upcoming event.

Eventually Betsy reworked her techno-bragging campaign, but it took a good six months to make up for lost time before she began to see her star rise again. Remember, telecommuting can be detrimental to your future only if you let it.

GET PERSONAL

"The only time I hear from him is when he wants to toot his own horn."

In my bragging workshops I often ask participants to recall the worst e-mail offenses in personal self-promotion they have encountered. The one complaint I hear frequently is being spammed by personal contacts. In a recent workshop, Marsha, a director of a major graphics design firm in Los Angeles, seemed to sum it up best with this story.

I don't want to sound like sour grapes. Usually I am totally jazzed when I hear from a friend or a colleague that their professional life is going well. This morning, in fact, one of my closest buddies, a commercial photographer, sent me a copy of an e-mail from the author of the book they just worked on together. I was thrilled for him and insisted we get together to celebrate.

But I have a friend, Charlie, whom I worked with for two years when we were starting out in the design field. We became good friends. When we parted ways for better opportunities, we used to call or correspond via e-mail to update each other on our pursuits. I moved up in the corporate world, while Charlie went off on his own as a freelancer. I hadn't heard from him for eighteen months, until recently, when he started sending me mass e-mail announcements every time he was quoted in the press, with some generic message like, "Just wanted you to see my tech-magazine article!" It makes me angry because I feel like he sees me as a business contact instead of a personal friend. If I were to hear from him at other times, even a holiday card, or if his announcements had a personal note at the top, even a line or two, it would be much easier to be happy for him.

Marsha now heads a department where the vast majority of the graphic work is assigned to freelancers. She adds, "Even though I could probably give Charlie a considerable amount of work, I won't because I am so put off by his self-congratulatory e-mails."

So add another quintessential brag bomb to your list: spamming business contacts with one-size-fits-all self-promotion. Don't let the efficiency of mass e-mail replace a little common sense, a little common courtesy, and the important personal side of communication—all key elements in mastering the art of techno-bragging.

BE CAREFUL WHAT YOU BRAG ABOUT

"His e-mail has come back to haunt him."

There is a fabulous line in the movie *State and Main* said by William H. Macy's character: "It's not a lie, it's a gift for fiction." Whether you opt for that definition or not, misrepresenting accomplishments, and not giving credit where credit is due, runs rampant in the corporate world.

So what does this have to do with techno-bragging? With e-mail increasingly becoming the favored way to communicate, I am happy to report that many corporate Pinocchios are getting caught, as they leave a mile-long paper trail bearing witness to their misdeeds. Brag hogs beware: As easy as it is to send an e-mail, it's just as easy for a recipient to forward it on. So you'd better start choosing your words wisely and share the credit, or like the fellow described below, you'll find your bragging bytes might come back to bite you.

"But . . . people only brag when they're insecure."

You're right about some people, but so what? They're not you and you're not insecure, so don't worry about it.

Jim, director of software development for a multimedia company, was under enormous pressure to correct major technical flaws in the company's core software in anticipation of a new competitor entering the market. After a meeting with the executive committee, Jim received a call from Aletha, the company's COO, suggesting that he contact an old friend of hers, an independent software developer, who was also working to solve technical problems very similar to those the company was facing.

Jim ignored her suggestion at first because, while Aletha was very successful on the operational side, she knew very little about the real nuts and bolts of building software. When she called back a week later to check up, Jim reluctantly proceeded to act on her suggestion. After much back-and-forth on the phone with Aletha's friend the developer, Jim met with him and was stunned to discover that the code the developer was working on would solve the company's problems almost immediately. Jim quickly set about putting together a potential deal to buy the exclusive software license, which would save the company another six months of work, nearly $2 million in development costs, and stop the competition in its tracks.

In his excitement Jim wrote a memo to the company's CEO outlining "his discovery" and the enormous advantages of the deal. The one small detail he left out, however, was Aletha's involvement. The CEO, thrilled with these latest developments, passed Jim's e-mail to the executive committee and board, praising his work. When Aletha got the e-mail she was furious at not being mentioned. Fortunately, she employed the twenty-four-hour rule: When you're angry with someone, give yourself a full day to calm down and collect yourself before responding so you don't regret what you say. But when she did finally speak to Jim, she let him know in no uncertain terms that he had misrepresented himself and that she wanted this corrected. Although Jim claimed he meant no harm, and that the oversight was unintended, the damage was there in black and white. It was going to take some time and real effort to undo. With his tail between his legs, Jim called the CEO to clarify the situation, admitting it was Aletha's idea in the first place. The CEO then sent out another correspondence saying, "It has come to my attention that our COO played a very important part in this upcoming deal. I'd like to thank Aletha for her initiative in putting us in contact with the developer on this deal, and remind everyone how important it is that we play as a team." Jim's oversight in the long run might appear inconsequential, but believe me, it wasn't. In fact, when it came time for Jim to be considered for the CTO position, the executive committee decided he needed more time to develop his leadership capabilities. *Ouch!*

CHAPTER 5

Job Interviews:
Bragging Your Way In the Door

- "It was awful! They questioned me about things I hadn't even thought of."
- "Why should I have to tell them? It's already on my résumé."
- "I have no experience—who would ever hire me?"
- "If you've been so successful on your own, why would you want to work for someone else?"
- "I know it may not look like it, but I'm perfect for this job."
- "How can I claim credit when my most impressive work experience is from a team effort?"
- "I don't know what to say when they ask for a reference from my last boss; frankly, she didn't like me."
- "So, tell us about your biggest weakness."
- "I have an MBA and five years of experience, but the clincher was something I hadn't expected."

Lights, camera, action! Take One. Nothing unnerves people more than job interviews. They're often the equivalent of an actor's audition: Recite a few lines. Sing a few bars. Next! Within seconds you're either praised or panned. Even oral surgery seems easier to get through. While a job interview is one of the few occasions completely set aside for no-holds-barred bragging, few people relish the notion of promoting themselves when they are being so blatantly sized up on the spot. To those who complain of feeling like trained seals: Guess what? It's not any easier on the other end. Given hour after hour of candidates reciting exactly what is on their résumés with no more animation than if they were reading the phone book, many employers and headhunters would rather spend the time having a few wisdom teeth extracted themselves.

What's wrong with this picture? Well, I hate to say this, but it's probably you! Last month I spoke to a forty-year-old, recently laid off communication director who was bemoaning the fact that she had sent out sixty résumés, gone on eight job interviews, and still hadn't snagged a position. As she explained to me the fierceness of the competition, because unemployed marketing professionals were a dime a dozen in this economy, I pulled out my "Take 12" questionnaire and simply asked her question #6, "What career successes are you most proud of having accomplished?" She paused and then stammered. Far from having an answer right there on the tip of her tongue—after eight interviews, no less—she proceeded to ramble on for about five minutes, never really answering the question. It was clear that the competition was not the real barrier: Her bragging campaign lacked preparation and focus.

When you are job hunting, the best way to prepare for interviews is to go back and review your answers to "Take 12." Write at the top of the page in large letters the five things about you that make you the perfect candidate for each position you have applied for. Focus on the experiences and strengths that best underscore why you are the best match for the job, and convey them in a way that helps the interviewer envision you in action. Pretend you were asked, "What would your current boss say about you?"—to which my friend Diane, an editor for a large daily newspaper, might respond, "He would say that I'm a pleasure to work with. We are under incredible deadlines in the newspaper business; things change on a dime. He likes my ability to turn things around fast, to get to the sources we need on a moment's notice, and to do so with a smile on my face."

Don't fudge your qualifications or describe yourself as someone you aren't. Stretching the truth makes people so anxious during job interviews that their own unease is what sinks them. When you choose words that honestly describe your strengths and experiences, reflecting a genuine belief that you are capable of doing a great job, it's infinitely easier to brag. And when you really believe in what you are saying, you're much more apt to relax, be conversational, and create a personal connection with the interviewer. My client Jean, for example, when applying for a sales position, was planning to pretend she had a stereotypical sales personality by using adjectives such as *outgoing, extroverted,* and *assertive.* I suggested instead that she fill her bragologues with descriptions of her authentic qualities, ones that would be equally useful for someone with sales responsibilities: enthusiasm, interest in the product, and liking to help people learn about things.

For any job interview, make sure to also prepare yourself for those zingers—the concerns that employers or headhunters might have about you and your career record. Develop responses that address a spotty job history, how your skills translate from one field to another, lack of experience, or those inevitable questions such as "Tell me about your weak points." Finally, on a separate piece of paper, write down everything you know about the organization and the people who will be at your interview— even if it requires lengthy online research, calling the human-resources director, or contacting a friend of a friend who might have the inside scoop. Check to ensure that your bragologue hits the target. Are the things you plan to say going to be exactly what the interviewer is likely to want to know about you? To help you out, the rest of this chapter is devoted to eye-opening stories of bragging bloopers and successes at job interviews and the lessons learned along the way.

DO YOUR HOMEWORK

"It was awful! They questioned me about things I hadn't even thought of."

Donna, marketing director for a Seattle-based health clinic, thought her interview for the position of development director for a prominent community arts center would be a cinch. After all, she had helped turn around a fledgling clinic, and patient enrollment was now at an all-time high. In addition, some fifteen years earlier she had been involved in the development of a well-known performing arts center in the Washington, D.C., area. Shopping for a new skirt and pair of heels for the big interview day, she breezed over in her mind her history and accomplishments, and felt comfortable that she would do just fine.

When she walked into the interview room, she was surprised to find the organization's six key players gathered around a conference room table waiting for her. Instead of one person interviewing her followed by another, the human-resources director explained, scheduling conflicts meant this was the only way to guarantee everyone who needed to meet her saw her. Like a storm approaching from afar on a sunny day, a feeling of dread quickly replaced Donna's easy attitude. Was this going to be an interview or an ambush?

Donna believed she got off to a good start as she outlined her marketing and sales successes with the health clinic. When they pressed her more, however, on how her health experience translated to increasing traffic and interest in the community arts center, things began to unravel. One of the directors pointed out that with lives on the line, people were more apt to invest in health care, whereas art was an entirely different matter. He reminded her of the center's slim operating budget. "I didn't realize that," she said, quietly berating herself for not digging out these details beforehand. When asked for some of her development ideas for the center, she continued, "Well, I'd really need to know more about your funding situation before I could discuss that. I was hoping we could do that today."

Her comment was met with chilly silence—one that said "Our purpose here today isn't to spend our time educating you, but rather to be enlightened by you."

Donna quickly redirected the conversation to her past experience in the performing arts, recalling some of the hurdles she overcame as the first assistant director at another center and a two-year stint as manager for a group of artists where she raised $500,000 in grants from the National Endowment for the Arts. That was all fine and dandy, but someone remarked that the world of fundraising was vastly different today from fifteen years ago. The NEA had become politicized and controversial, fallen victim to some huge funding cuts, and had become a very unreliable source of funds for smaller organizations. They had learned long ago to place their bets elsewhere. This person asked her whether she knew other private foundations in the region that could support the organization. Someone pointed out that the first two she mentioned as potential sources were already contributors, something she had read on the organization's website but had forgotten. As she stumbled through the rest of the meeting, she looked out on a sea of glazed stares and thought "How could this cinch of an interview have sunk so low?"

To her credit, though, instead of skulking away and hiding under the covers for the next two days, she called back one woman on the interviewing committee whom she knew from a board they had once served on together. Admitting that she was not happy with the interview, Donna asked if she could come back and present a full-fledged development plan. The woman agreed and Donna took advantage of her second chance not only by crafting a bang-up development proposal but by getting all her bragging ducks in a row.

DON'T LET YOUR RÉSUMÉ SPEAK FOR YOU

"Why should I have to I tell them? It's already on my résumé."

Last year my nephew Max, who had just graduated from college, returned to Philadelphia to look for a job. His days were devoted to the hunt, while evenings he worked as a bartender. Before he contacted me for advice, he had attended eight informational and four actual job interviews but had come up empty-handed. I was surprised to hear this. Max had been an excellent student and had completed two high-profile internships a few summers before, one with the mayor's office. Something wasn't right. At the urging of his increasingly nervous mom, he called Aunt Peggy before his next important meeting with a prospective employer.

When he finally reached me, I suggested we try a mock interview, which I opened up by asking, "So tell me about some of your work with the city."

"Well," said Max, "two years ago, I completed a summer internship with the mayor's Business Action Team, his personal arm of the commerce department. I got to do some different things in helping the city retain and attract businesses." End of story.

"Max, is that it? Or is this just a bad cell phone connection?" I asked.

"Yeah, that's about it, Aunt Peggy, at least for that question," he replied.

"But . . . what I did was really nothing. I don't want to come off like I'm making a mountain out of a molehill."

Okay, *you* might think it's nothing, but I'll bet a lot of others would think it's *something*. Don't sell yourself short by underestimating the value of what you do.

"Really? I remember you telling me about a whole bunch of interesting projects you were doing for that commission. Why don't you take me through them?"

"They're on my résumé—do you want me to shoot you a copy?" he asked.

"No, Max," I said, "I want you to talk about them and bring them to life."

"Well, here, I'll read it to you," he said, proceeding to robotically recap his résumé. And therein lay the problem. Max, like many other college graduates, had sunk hundreds of dollars into getting his résumé just right. He had devoted all of his job preparation to the written word. As a result, he assumed his résumé should do most of the talking. I asked, "If all employers wanted was for you to read your résumé to them, why do you think they would bother to meet you?" I reminded him that employers weren't psychics, and explained the purpose of an interview was for them to get to know him, see what he was like, and hear the story of his accomplishments. I added,

"Your résumé doesn't have your sparkling personality and energy. You need to show employers how you would be a great asset to their firm because of the experience you've had and your enthusiasm for the position."

Taking great liberties as his aunt, I continued, "Moreover, you sound like you are snoozing your way through this mock interview instead of schmoozing. Your energy is low. Your voice is a monotone. You sound bored with yourself, and you're boring me. So get up off your tush and pump up the passion. Start walking around the room and get some blood flowing to your brain. But before you start telling me again about this fabulous experience you had working with the mayor, I want you to say to yourself in a very exaggerated manner: *I am so excited to be here. I can't wait to tell you about my experiences, and you would be absolutely crazy not to hire me!*"

There was a long pause. "Okay, Aunt Peggy, give me a moment," he said. (I told you he was smart, didn't I?) He then launched full throttle into a very detailed story about his summer internship with the mayor's special arm of the commerce division. He talked about helping small businesses cut through the red tape at City Hall for services, and about how he was part of a team that enticed three large companies to relocate to the city, adding millions in tax revenues. Barely stopping for breath, he bridged that experience to his most recent summer job, dropping the name of his boss, a well-known commercial developer acclaimed for his urban work reviving two depressed downtown neighborhoods. He delivered additional brag bites about his research scouting out large abandoned lots for revitalization and their impact on communities and the environment. Max ended by saying how exciting it had been to report his findings to the developer and how he had even played Ansel Adams, taking stunning photographs of the depressed sites ripe for renewal and incorporating them into his various presentations. His knowledge, his wit, his passion for urban renewal came through loud and clear. I wasn't surprised when he called me the next afternoon to say he had been asked back for round two. One more interview after that and he landed the job. I considered taking 10 percent of his first year's salary, but Max swears he'll take care of me in my old age.

GET CREATIVE

"I have no experience—who would ever hire me?"

Aileen, a soon-to-be economics graduate from Wharton, came to me for interview coaching. She was concerned that she had no corporate experience to land a job on Wall Street. I had to agree with her on that score. Fortunately she was graduating from a highly regarded college where she had excelled in her studies. Her grade point average was high, and two of her economics professors had written letters of referral praising the research she had conducted for her senior thesis on the emergence of microcredit in underdeveloped nations. She could certainly draw on her successes from college, but what was missing was the hook for her story—the reason she had a passion for the financial side of business to begin with.

"Why are you interested in Wall Street?" I asked her.

"I've always liked working with numbers" was her response. Imagining how far an answer like that would get her on a job interview, I said, "Aileen, isn't there *anything* that sparked your interest in the financial side of business, like running a lemonade stand or something?"

"Well, yeah, I guess so," she said.

It all started with my grandfather, who founded and ran one of the largest retail stores in the Southwest. From the age of twelve, I spent my Saturdays and summers working for him until I went to college. I would have gone back to work with him more, but he passed away and the business was sold. When I first started, I did small jobs like stocking the shelves, sweeping the floors, and showing customers where to find what they were looking for. By age fourteen, I was running one of the registers, and a year later, overseeing all the clerks. Eventually I moved on to inventory—taking it and figuring out how much we had to order each season based on previous years' sales and the local economy. My grandfather taught me accounting, and by the time I went to college I was already doing much of his bookkeeping. Come to think of it, I was really a financial analyst even back then.

Now we were getting somewhere! So in her next interview Aileen said this:

My passion for economics and the financial side of business started at the ripe old age of twelve. I worked in my grandfather's retail store on Saturdays and during summer breaks. It was quite a large operation in Tucson that sold everything from panty hose to peanuts. I started with stocking the shelves, moved on to the register, and then inventory control. By the age of sixteen, I was pretty much handling the accounting and bookkeeping. I was a financial analyst in the making. My grandfather taught me everything. He would have been so proud of me graduating from Wharton with a degree in economics with honors.

Something must have worked. Aileen got her first job on Wall Street two months later.

ZAP THOSE ZINGERS

"If you've been so successful on your own, why would you want to work for someone else?"

Bernice, age fifty, has spent the last twenty-five years working for herself as a management consultant for family foundations. Although highly successful, she wanted to return to a more traditional job in the corporate world. On one of her first job interviews, she found her heart stop when one of the partners asked her point-blank, "If you've been so successful on your own, why would you want to work for someone else?" This is when she felt herself slipping into defensive mode and, as she tried to justify her success, her responses became increasingly curt.

"What was the real truth?" I asked her. She told me that it was simply because working from home had allowed her the flexibility to care for her children, while at the same time earning a living. Now that they were grown, she was ready to spread her wings again. Together we worked on a good way to answer the question so it no longer stopped her in her tracks. The new bragologue went like this:

> I have been working in the field of philanthropy for twenty-five years. When I had my last child seventeen years ago, I realized that my job demanded too much travel and too many late nights for a mother of three. So I left the company and went out on my own, to have more control over my schedule. I had planned all along to return to a firm when the youngest left home. D-Day is about to happen this fall, so I am taking the step that I always knew I would. I have really enjoyed running my own business and have learned a lot of things about myself, my values, my boundaries, and of course, managing profit-and-loss statements. I'm lucky to have been successful while enjoying each and every one of the families and foundations I've worked with. Now I want to use my skills on a broader stage, which I think a larger organization will give me. Believe it or not, I am actually looking forward to the travel. Isn't that ironic, given that most of my friends have been on and off planes for the last twenty years and are ready to stay at home?

Fortunately for Bernice, she didn't have to suffer through more than one heart-stopping experience to realize that she had to prepare and practice for this inevitable fastball.

By her second interview, however, she was zapping that zinger with a carefully constructed bragologue. As of this writing she is deciding between two offers.

MAKE THE LEAP

"I know it may not look like it, but I'm perfect for this job."

Howard was one of my very first clients on Wall Street. Three years ago, he decided to leave that world, where he had spent thirteen years as head of a multimillion-dollar research department, to work in the nonprofit field. First, however, he took two years off and fulfilled his dream of writing and publishing the Greek version of *Roots*, a cultural travelogue tracing the stories his grandmother had shared with him growing up.

When he reemerged in search of nonprofit work, he knew it wasn't going to be a walk in the park. He figured he had six strikes against him: (1) He was a middle-aged guy. (2) He had taken off a chunk of time at an age when people are expected to be seriously into their careers. (3) He was switching to a field in which he had no formal experience. (4) The country was in the middle of one of the worst recessions ever, meaning that few were hiring. (5) He was going to have to beat down the stereotype of an insensitive corporate "slasher," as he moved from one of the most cutthroat industries on earth to the more benign and gentlemanly nonprofit world. (6) He had to overcome his reluctance to toot his own horn.

A self-confessed introvert, Howard was one of the smartest and most accomplished professionals I had ever met, yet I had always had to drag every good deed out of him. Despite these formidable odds, we worked together taking a full inventory of his skills, personality, and history. We filled his brag bag with brag bites and bragologues galore, so that he came to the interviewing arena fully armed.

"But . . . you don't need to brag if you can deliver."

Oy, this makes me crazy! It makes no sense. Why do people say this? Does it mean that anyone who talks about something she has accomplished is incompetent? Puh-leeeze.

As we'd predicted, the interviews always started off with zingers like, "So why do you want go into the nonprofit world when you will be paid half to two-thirds less than what you made on Wall Street?" Instead of getting defensive, he calmly answered, "At this point in my life, I am lucky to have made enough money and am comfortable with taking a salary cut." He always added, "I realized how much I wanted to do this kind of work when I looked back at the last five years and noticed that I had spent all my free time outside of the office working with nonprofit groups. I was an active member of one board and became a management consultant to two others. I helped them design and stick to a budget, hire administrative staff, and implement their technology systems. I was also able to use my IT background, having developed the first web library in the early nineties—unheard of even in financial firms—which I managed to build with just ten people and roll out globally six months ahead of schedule to thirty-five thousand clients." He then further quelled their fears by adding that he would not be the nonprofit Al Dunlap. "At my old job I was charged with reducing the budget for analysts' reports by fifty million dollars. I did it without firing a single soul; instead, I found more cost-efficient ways to do the research and print the reports." They got it: If he could deliver for a large firm, he could be effective with an organization one-sixteenth its size.

STAR PLAYER VS. TEAM SPIRIT

"How can I claim credit when my most impressive work experience is from a team effort?"

A client of mine, who worked as an assistant brand manager for a packaged-goods company, felt uncomfortable taking credit for successful sales force initiatives because he had played only a small part in a much larger collaborative effort. I recommended that he break down the project into ten parts that were all key to the project's success, then asked him to talk about the two or three he was the most involved in, being sure to underscore the team effort. His bragologue sounded like this:

I grew up eating so much Cap'n Crunch that I could have joined CEA, Cereal Eaters Anonymous, so I was in heaven in my last position launching a new breakfast cereal. What's more, I was fortunate to work with an amazing group of colleagues and was able to learn so much more from the collaboration than I ever would have on my own. The team leader had twenty years of experience in the ready-to-eat-cereal industry and was a wonderful mentor. By the end of the project, I felt like I had soaked up at least half of those years just from working so closely with her! I was responsible for managing the research and sales data and creating all of our reports. It's really important to me that information is presented in a clear and concise manner and that reports have an attractive and simple-to-follow appearance. During the project I received many compliments on my work from the manager and from my colleagues. Our company president sent an e-mail congratulating all of us when the project was completed, and he specifically mentioned how much he liked the format of the final report, which I had produced.

TRUTH TRICKS

"I don't know what to say when they ask for a reference from my last boss; frankly, she didn't like me."

Okay, so you and your boss never bonded. She didn't like you much and you were not crazy about her. Still, you can turn this to your brag advantage as Jessica learned to do. When she no longer could stand working for her high-strung, demanding boss, who'd had it in for her from Day One, Jessica walked away from her job of two years as an advertising representative. This is the bragologue she developed to zap the zinger:

> I learned a lot from Bonnie and developed my skills a tremendous amount, but eventually I outgrew the position and wanted a job with more responsibilities. I had expanded my client base to three times the size of when I first started and held the top two accounts in the firm. I was ready for bigger challenges; I wanted to manage projects and really test my expertise. To be candid, Bonnie and I had differences of opinion about how things should be done, and so she is not the best person to ask for a reference. I do, however, have three other colleagues, one of whom is a founding partner at the firm. She would be happy to talk with you about my work.

BRAGGING THROUGH YOUR WEAK POINTS

"So tell us about your biggest weakness."

You should be prepared to answer this perennial favorite of seemingly every interviewer, one that is sure to get you squirming in your chair. The best way to respond is to gracefully acknowledge a liability, while spinning it as having a positive side with benefits that far outweigh the negatives. For example, my friend Lynn readily admits that having too much energy is her biggest weakness. In an interview, her bragologue should sound like this:

Some people might say that I have too much energy. And it's true that being so energetic makes me prone to think I can do everything by myself. I have been known to take on too many tasks without delegating. Then when I get pressed for time, I can begin to talk so fast that I sound like Alvin the chipmunk. On the positive side, I get an amazing amount of things done. I can multi-task with the best of them, and at the end of a major project I don't need much downtime to recover. Fortunately my high energy level is accompanied by a positive disposition and the optimism needed to see even challenging projects through to completion.

THERE IS NO SUCH THING AS A SMALL DETAIL

"I have an MBA and five years of experience, but the clincher was something I hadn't expected."

Jennifer, a thirty-one-year-old analyst in the food industry, had been wanting for some time to make a move to the booming natural-foods sector when a ripe opportunity presented itself. Even though she had no professional experience in this industry niche, Jennifer's brag bag was filled with natural-food nuggets from her personal history that she could leverage to show the company why they were a perfect match for each other. In her cover letter she talked about growing up in the health-food store that her mother owned, testing recipes in college for a famous natural-foods cookbook author, and nurturing a lifelong interest in organic farming. That, combined with a finely tuned résumé, seemed to do the trick. Within days she was asked to a screening interview with the HR director, followed by a callback with the person who would be her boss, then invited to meet with the company president. Each person asked Jennifer whether she had experience in the natural-products industry and she said, "Well, I did grow up in a health-food store!" And each interviewer replied, "Oh yeah, I remember that from your cover letter." This moment became the springboard for Jennifer to mention how her early experiences with the family business led to a lifelong interest in health and nutrition as well. A seemingly little detail about growing up in a health-food store quickly developed into mythic proportions because her boss, it turned out, mentioned it in his all-points e-mail announcing her hire. As Jennifer recalls, "The first week on the job, it seemed that everyone I met brought it up to me, saying something like, 'I hear you were the health-foods poster child. So tell me, what was it like growing up in your mother's store?' Who would have thought that such a personal detail would end up carrying the day?"

Crafting creative, memorable messages and stories about yourself and accomplishments is at the heart of your bragging campaign. A good preparation technique is to have a friend conduct a mock interview with you and to tape it on video. On playback, examine how you come across, concentrating on whether what you are saying sounds unique, interesting, credible, and compelling. Does it distinguish you from the pack of others who are applying for the same job? If you think someone else could just as easily be telling your story, it's time to dig deeper for the golden nuggets that will set you apart.

CHAPTER 6

◎

Performance Reviews: The Good, the Bad, and the Ugly

- "Help! My performance review is tomorrow."
- "I was all ready to ask for a raise and promotion, but I lost my nerve."
- "Oh, it was really nothing."
- "He told me everything great he had accomplished since the last review, but none of it was part of his actual job."
- "He was stuck on these two little things and it drove me nuts."
- "The last thing I want to do in a performance review is call attention to my weak points."

Lights, camera, action! Take Two. Performance reviews are right up there next to job interviews as the least favorite pastime for professionals. The challenge of convincing others you should get the job is now replaced with the challenge of convincing them that they have made the right choice. Despite managers finding them a chore and

employees considering them torture, performance reviews
are the perfect opportunity to turn up the volume on your
career.

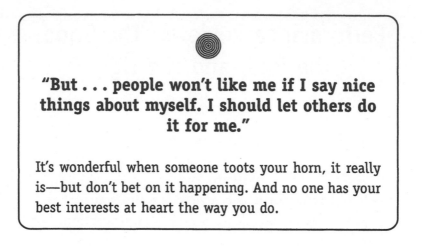

**"But . . . people won't like me if I say nice
things about myself. I should let others do
it for me."**

It's wonderful when someone toots your horn, it really
is—but don't bet on it happening. And no one has your
best interests at heart the way you do.

It's never too early to start planning for your next performance review. If you've kept your brag bag up to date
with a record of your accomplishments and milestones—
and you've engaged in an ongoing performance review for
yourself by strategically bragging all year long—then getting ready for your performance review will be easy. If not,
you've got your work cut out for you. You'll need to out-
line your progress since taking the job, or your last review,
and assemble hard data that demonstrates what you've already done for the company and how you will do even
more in the future. You see, when you don't keep a log of
your accomplishments, you're more apt to forget the
specifics that speak volumes about your value. And if you
try to reconstruct a year's worth of projects, successes, and

challenges in the midst of the review, it's unlikely you'll be able to put on your best performance.

Today companies use all sorts of performance-review tools, but no matter what the tool, the best performance reviews let managers and employees have an honest two-way discussion about an employee's milestones, mistakes, and areas for improvement. Don't make the mistake of letting your manager do all the talking while you sit passively by and listen. It's up to you to take the initiative and make sure your boss hears what you want him or her to hear.

DON'T WING IT

"Help! My performance review is tomorrow."

Why do people wait until the day before their performance review to prepare? We so dread sitting in that hot seat that we'd rather take our chances and wing it. Well, you know the old wing-it rule, don't you? Twenty percent of the time when you wing it, you do succeed in communicating what you need to in a very effective manner; the other 80 percent of the time you don't. The worst thing you can do is walk into a performance review cold. Even lukewarm isn't such a good idea. You need to be *hot* and fearlessly say what you have to without hemming and hawing, shuffling your feet, lowering your gaze, or becoming tongue-tied. Putting your brag bag in order prepares you to present yourself in the most positive light possible and to address any concerns your boss might raise.

"I am amazed at how lackadaisical some employees are when it comes to performance reviews," says Paul, the vice president of creative services at an Internet start-up, who reviews eight employees every quarter. "They see the whole process as burdensome, rather than an opportunity to take the spotlight, talk about their accomplishments, and spend some quality time with the boss discussing their future. They put so little time into the written self-evaluation—which they pass in at the last minute, leaving me no time to absorb it. And then they come into my office and sit there expecting *me* to do all the talking. Instead of being a dialogue, it's a one-way monologue of me basically spewing out what I expect of them. It's really quite simple: The ones who spend time preparing for performance reviews are the ones who get my attention. I just see them as more committed to their careers and the company's future."

Kimberly, a twenty-eight-year-old computer analyst, is a perfect example of a winger. I had just finished coaching her for an upcoming trade speech when she dropped the bomb that her performance review was scheduled in two days and, by the way, could we spend the final fifteen minutes of our session getting her ready for it? Okey-dokey, I thought, this was going to require some speed-talking on my part. "What are three things you've accomplished since your last performance review and what are your key goals for the next six months?" I asked.

Usually a chatterbox, Kimberly was speechless—not a good sign. Apparently she hadn't given the review a single moment's thought until now. I continued, "Name three ways that you have improved the company's bottom line, either through increased revenues or savings."

Uh-oh, now she was in deer-caught-in-the-headlights

mode. I added, thinking that if I asked enough questions I might hit an answer, "What are some examples of positive client feedback, either written or verbal, that reflect on your contributions?"

"Ah-ha," she said. "The Olsen account manager said I had single-handedly saved the project."

"Do you have that in writing?" I asked.

"No," she responded, "but I'll call the account manager today and see if she'll e-mail a note describing my contributions." Now she was finally waking up.

"Kimberly, what do you want to walk out of your review with—a better title, a new job description, more staff, a bigger office, more money?"

She smiled and said, "I hope, at a minimum, they'll increase my salary. I've been putting in a lot of extra hours!"

Hope, I told her, wasn't going to carry her performance appraisal or ensure a fatter paycheck, but better preparation would.

The preliminary work is critical to a successful performance appraisal; so is how well you communicate and interact with your manager. Create and rehearse a conversational bragologue that sums up your positive contributions, including concrete examples of your strengths. Get ready for the zingers, those questions that can throw you off-balance, such as, "In what area do you need the most improvement?" Recognize that it takes time to get ready for a performance review. Treat it as one of the most important moments in your career—with the same level of attention and enthusiasm you gave to landing the job in the first place.

STICK TO YOUR GUNS

"I was all ready to ask for a raise and promotion, but I lost my nerve."

Your bragologues are ready, you're raring to go, you sit down at your performance review, and what happens? Your boss cuts you off, your review gets sidetracked, and before you know it, you are scratching your head wondering why that carefully planned bragging campaign never got off the ground.

Andy, a young associate in private banking, was looking forward to his performance review. He had had a stellar year and was exceeding his previous numbers, despite the recession. He had all his bragging ducks in a row, ready to fire away, but he never got off the first shot.

His boss opened the performance review by saying, "Andy, you have done a good job this year. As you know, however, this has been a tough year in the financial markets. I've just come from a meeting, where word is that bonuses will be off about forty percent. And we aren't out of the woods yet. We are probably going to go through another round of layoffs."

Suddenly Andy stopped thinking about the bonus and promotion he had spent hours preparing to ask for, and started thinking how lucky he felt to even have a job. Asking for a promotion at that moment, much less a raise, seemed not only self-centered but also pointless. Instead of rolling out his carefully planned bragologues about client satisfaction, new business won, professional development, the VP title, and his bonus, Andy spent the rest of his performance review talking about what was on his boss' mind. Wasn't it better, he thought, to be a team player and use the time to schmooze with her about the division's survival, than to selfishly talk about his personal situation?

A few hours later, as Andy was looking back at his so-called review, the whole experience began to gnaw at him. He found himself becoming increasingly upset at having been denied the opportunity to be heard. I was glad we worked together soon after this happened because we were able to channel Andy's resentment. I advised him to immediately make another appointment to see his boss, explaining to her that he wanted to discuss a few things they hadn't had a chance to cover at the performance review. Andy agreed to call the boss, rather than wait the six months until his next review date, and they scheduled a meeting for the following week. Andy was nervous! So we practiced his opening bragologue to increase his comfort level and an inner monologue to increase his sense of urgency. As he walked from his desk to the boss' office on the day of the follow-up review, he repeatedly ran the inner monologue through his mind: "I can't wait to tell you about all the exciting things that have been happening!" And when he reached her office, this is what he said:

I know the firm is suffering, and everyone is going to take a hit, but I feel really good about *my* business and how my hard work over the last three years is finally paying off. This year, I was able to bring in my two largest clients after a year and a half of nurturing the deals. My revenues are *up* twenty percent, which is great at any time, and even more so now that most bankers' are *down* thirty percent. Also, I really took

your advice at my last performance review to heart
and have become more active in the firm. I have organized monthly breakfasts for our business referrals
so that they can learn about our new products, which
has been very well received. Deborah, the division
head, just sent me an e-mail thanking me for my efforts. For all of these reasons, I think I am ready for
the vice-president title and would like to see a bonus
that reflects my accomplishments, despite the dismal
state of affairs.

Andy's boss asked some follow-up questions, which he
was well prepared to answer. Two months later, when the
rest of Andy's team got a mere 40 percent of last year's
bonus, Andy's was reduced only 10 percent. Not bad for a
recession. And about four months later, he was named VP.

LEARN HOW TO ACCEPT COMPLIMENTS

"Oh, it was really nothing."
    "You did a nice job organizing the seminar last fall," said
Barbara's boss as he looked over her written self-evaluation
in her performance review.
    "Don't mention it," she replied.
    "I thought it was remarkable that we got the chief econ-
omist from Tampa to fly in for it," her boss continued.
    "My stars were aligned that day. He was going to be in
the area anyway that week," Barbara said, her words followed by a girlish giggle.

"I think it's one of the best conferences we've given to the group in three years," added her boss.

"Do you really think so?" she asked, drawing into question her own self-worth and accomplishments.

"I wouldn't be saying so if I didn't think so," her boss responded, a bit perturbed with Barbara's coyness.

I don't know which people shy away from more: criticism or compliments. The next time you give someone a compliment, watch his reaction. Rarely does he take it in, absorb the meaning, and answer fully, "Thank you, I really appreciate your saying that," or "Thank you, that means a lot coming from you." Instead he guffaws, clears his throat, shuffles his feet, hangs his head, or childishly giggles. Then more often than not, he proceeds to minimize or deny the compliment or chalk it up to being lucky. Women especially are notorious for deflecting compliments, even going so far as to turn a compliment around to insult themselves. For example, how many times have you heard someone tell a woman, "You look great," only to hear in response, "Really? I'd look better if only I could lose another ten pounds!"

In performance reviews it's important to turn compliments into launching pads for underscoring your hard work and aspirations. This is what Barbara could have said in response to her boss' positive feedback:

Boss: You did a nice job organizing the seminar last fall.

Barbara: Thank you. I'm glad you feel that way, because it's the feedback everyone else has given me as well. In fact, I brought along some of the letters of thanks we received from the clients who are already eager for next year's conference. And even though the next conference is six months away, it's already sixty percent booked!

Boss: I thought it was quite remarkable that we got the chief economist from Tampa to fly in for it.

Barbara: I know. I was really pleased that he was able to do it. But it wasn't a surprise! For the last couple of years, I've gone out of my way to develop a relationship with him, knowing how important it is to have good speakers. In fact, I've already lined up some of the top experts in the automotive field for our upcoming event in Detroit.

Boss: I think it's one of the best conferences we've given to the group in three years.

Barbara: Me too! I wasn't so sure when I got Dick's message saying he was snowed in at Denver and couldn't make the opening-day panel, but then everyone else we had was so impressive it didn't matter. From that point on, I knew it was going to be great. So with this now fresh in our minds, I'd like you to consider letting me handle the conference in Asia. I know it's the company's largest event, but I assisted on it last year and I'm sure I can make it a great success.

Embracing a compliment is akin to learning how to feel comfortable bragging about yourself. Accepting a compliment doesn't mean you're conceited; rather, it means you have a healthy self-image and are a valuable person who deserves credit. Throwing a compliment back makes the sender feel uncomfortable and wonder why she had even bothered. Deflecting a compliment by reducing or denying it makes the sender far less likely to throw one your way again. An effective self-promoter accepts a compliment graciously, often by looking the complimenter in the eye while simply saying "Thank you" with a smile. If the situation permits, you will also use it as a springboard to sincerely showcase the hard work that went into reaching your goals. Don't giggle a compliment away; smile it in.

BRAG ABOUT THE RIGHT STUFF

"He told me everything great he had accomplished since the last review, but none of it was part of his actual job."

"I spent major time with the IT department, helping them get some of the bugs out of our new software upgrade," said Jerry to his boss, suggesting that without his input the $200,000 upgrade would have gone up in smoke.

"I organized the company's softball team this year, and as you know, we won the league championship for the first time ever," Jerry added later, giving his boss a blow-by-blow description of the championship game.

"I really helped some of the others over rough spots in their assignments," Jerry said, revealing that he had completely opened up his Rolodex, sharing his sources on some key stories.

These bragologues would be perfectly acceptable except for a few important facts: Jerry is a journalist for a national trade publication. His main responsibility is to report on the construction and building sector. This discussion is taking place during his annual performance review, and he's tooting his horn about everything except what he has accomplished as it relates to his position and responsibilities.

The strangest thing about this story is that Jerry actually has a lot to brag about when it comes to his core job achievements. According to his boss, the senior editor, who approached me about improving the company's employee appraisal process, "Jerry has scooped the competition on several occasions. He landed exclusive interviews with some of the key players in our sector. But instead of talking about those accomplishments or his plans for the future, Jerry blabbed on and on about his peripheral deeds. I didn't want to insult him by interrupting, so I stayed the course. But before I knew it, our forty-five minutes were up."

Jerry would have been far more effective in his performance review had he first crafted a bragologue to address the basics. He could have said, "Since my last review, one of the key goals has been for the magazine to become number one in the design-build trade, and I've pushed the envelope on the editorial side to do this. I'm not only all over a story when it breaks, like with my reporting of the Sinchaw debacle, but also way ahead of the curve, which you saw with my story on the controversial industrial park."

Even in a performance review, you need to be strategic about what you brag about and to prioritize your accomplishments. While it's fine to toot about the extras you do on the side, don't forget to cover your "mission critical" accomplishments: how you have succeeded in the job you were hired to do, how you have contributed to the goals of your boss and the company, and how you have addressed any concerns raised in your last performance review.

HELP YOUR BOSS SEE THE FOREST THROUGH THE TREES

"He was stuck on these two little things and it drove me nuts."

Six months ago you saved the day with a brilliant idea for a new advertising campaign. Three months ago you worked weekends gathering information for a new business pitch, a multimillion-dollar account the company landed. But all your manager can remember is this: For the last two weeks you've been late getting into the office. It's true you've never been the most punctual person, and the last two weeks have been worse than usual.

So how do you keep your cool and go on to remind your boss of what you've done during the rest of the year? One of the purposes of filling up your brag bag before a performance review is to boost your confidence so you'll be able to take criticism without wilting. If you fire back with denials or interrupt with a lot of "but this–but that," the situation is likely to escalate into a shouting match.

The best way to respond to performance review criticisms is to acknowledge each shortcoming with a reminder of your strengths. For example, Susan, an assistant account executive in advertising, who had been late the last few weeks, replied, "Yes, I have been late recently and I apologize for any inconvenience it may have caused. I'm a new parent and went through a change in my daycare situation, but now things are ironed out. For the most part, though, I have always been available at the flip of a switch and completely committed to our work. As you may recall, during my pregnancy leave I worked several weekends to help with that new business pitch when you were short on staff. It paid off. Our campaign was brilliant and strategically well-positioned."

"But . . . I met my numbers. What else matters?"

Numbers aren't enough! Colleagues and bosses want to know how you got there, not just what you've got.

The worse thing you can do is turn up the heat in a performance review by getting defensive and emotional. So here are my brag nags for staying calm and collected in a difficult situation: Take a deep breath, count to ten, accept your shortcomings, offer thanks for the constructive feedback, gently focus on your strong points, and help your manager see the bigger picture. Be sure to ask for specific and measurable goals to improve your performance, so that next time you can brag about having achieved them.

LEARN TO ASK THE HARD QUESTIONS ABOUT YOURSELF

"The last thing I want to do in a performance review is call attention to my weak points."

Is getting no bad news in your performance review good news? Many managers dread performance reviews and having to tell employees how their work either fit the bill or didn't. They fear the conflict and worry about damaging work relationships. Afraid of offending, many dance around the real issues and the areas of needed improvement. Preferring to stay in the safe zone, they focus the appraisal on an employee's strengths rather than weaknesses. So what's so bad about that? Well, if you shy away from finding out what's really on their minds, you might miss the chance to correct their misconceptions or to develop steps for improving the situation.

Leah, a real estate broker for a nationwide firm, has received positive performance reviews for the last year. Her promotion to head of office is considered a sure thing. So you can imagine her surprise when she hears she has been passed over for the promotion. She marches into her boss' office and he proceeds to tell her that, when it came down to the final decision, the executive committee called her leadership and interpersonal skills into question. Leah was completely dumbfounded. These issues hadn't even come up in her performance review. Since she assumed her promotion was on track, Leah hadn't bothered to keep her boss up to speed on her latest initiatives. So she proceeded to describe to him how she had gotten involved in the company's mentoring program three months ago, completely taking on two new hires, walking them through the company listing process, introducing them to agents from competing firms, bringing them with her to closings, and providing them with a list of amenities in each area. Leah had also recently volunteered to work on the firm's growth-opportunity committee. Once she had reminded her boss of her accomplishments, he readily offered a sincere apology for overlooking them and promised to bring them to the attention of the executive committee the next time around.

As for her interpersonal skills, Leah claimed she had never been told of any problems in this area. Later, however, she admitted to me, "Okay, I've run into a few rough spots with people in the customer-relations department, but my boss never brought them up and I didn't want to mention them either. I mean, who wants to underscore their weak points in a performance review? It's up to the boss." I pointed out to Leah that it was their mutual responsibility to talk about areas needing improvement, and the fact that they weren't brought up in the review preceding a possible promotion to a management position was a huge oversight on both their parts. Actually, when you're deficient in an area but can demonstrate with a well-thought-out bragologue how you have improved, even your weak points can add up to a plus!

A few days later Leah called her boss and asked for a *real* performance review. Now that the cat was out of the bag, her boss discussed honestly how her directness was sometimes perceived as overly aggressive and was a turnoff to others. They agreed that Leah would enroll in a management training class and they would strategize together about other high-visibility opportunities she should pursue within the company to showcase her leadership abilities and newfound management skills. In the end, even with the good, the bad, and the ugly, it turned out to be the most constructive performance review she had ever received.

CHAPTER 7

———————◎———————

When You Don't Have a "Real" Job

- "So, what do *YOU* do?"
- "I don't know what to say about myself because I'm not sure what I want to do."
- "I may be retired, but don't count me out."
- "The truth is, I'm not doing anything that would impress anyone."
- "I had a hard time getting her past the cupcakes."

When you don't have a "real" job, whether by choice or default, it's easy to feel like there's nothing exciting about you that's worth bragging about.

More than most of us will admit, our identities are tied up in our jobs and careers. For proof, just go to a cocktail party or friendly neighborhood barbecue. When meeting someone new, the first question typically asked is, "What do you do?" which, loosely translated, means, "How do you get the money to support yourself or family?" If you are unemployed, without a snappy bragologue comeback, watch how quickly the conversation disintegrates and the other party starts looking over your shoulder, ready to move on to someone more interesting. Without an up-to-date brag bag, your self-esteem and confidence hang precariously in the balance, leaving you with that uneasy feeling of being undervalued, boring, invisible, and disconnected.

Careers today are no longer set in stone. More professionals than ever before are stepping out of the workforce for a variety of reasons. For some it's permanent, but for many others it's a hiatus that can last anywhere from a few months to a few years or even more. You might be a mom or dad jumping off the fast track to care for the kiddies, planning to return one day; a retiree not altogether sure you are really ready to call it quits; an "in-betweener," looking for a job without a current one, fighting postlay-off blues; or a "corporate dropout," taking time off to smell the roses while considering your next move. Whatever your situation, whatever your timetable, whatever your plans (and especially if you don't have any yet!), you must overcome the tendency to remove yourself from the bragging loop. Regardless what direction your life is taking, continue to self-promote. You can never be sure what's around the next bend or where the next opportunity might come from.

The first step in rebuilding a brag campaign is to refresh your memory of "what's so good about you" by reviewing your answers to the "Take 12" survey. Remind yourself that not having a "real" job doesn't erase your entire past or diminish what you are doing now. Look at how your past accomplishments and your current situation might tie in to future goals. Begin to formulate catchy bragologues and brag bites that can strategically plant seeds for future growth opportunities. Whether or not you know what the next move is, everyone needs an upbeat "act as if everything is going great" story about the current stage of life. Think of interesting and exciting ways to describe what you are up to now that are appealing to different mindsets. The last thing people want to hear is doom-and-gloom stories filled with self-doubt, unless of course they're your best friend, or a therapist who gets paid to listen! You don't want people to feel sorry for you; you want them to get excited about you.

KNOW WHAT TO LEAVE OUT

"So what do YOU *do?"*

It's difficult to respond to this seemingly simple question when there is no simple answer. Fewer and fewer career paths proceed in a linear fashion. They can be as complex as they are colorful. It takes preparation and focus to determine which hot buttons to hit and which ones to ignore when you've got thirty seconds to answer that what-do-you-do question.

My mind was wandering to the buffet table and refills on the guacamole. I had been standing for almost ten minutes, unable to politely break away from the conversation for reasons that will become evident in a minute, and along with my growing impatience, my stomach was beginning to growl. I was at a friend's engagement party in New York, and I'd made the mistake of asking Jeri, a friend of the bride's, what she did for a living. I had heard she was quite accomplished, at one point having been the public affairs director for one of the boroughs. I thought she would be interesting to talk to, but our conversation was proving otherwise. Ten sentences into her bragologue—if you can call it that—I completely lost track of the story. Her vague and rambling description was making it challenging for me to stay attentive. The only thing coming through loud and clear was that she was unhappily in between jobs. Jeri knew I was an executive coach, which people often assume is a green light to tell all, as if they were talking to their hairdresser or therapist. I tried not to rudely cut into her one-way snoreologue, now going into what felt like the eleventh inning of a baseball game with no end in sight. I was beginning to wonder if the communication field was really her true calling.

A pause in the conversation allowed me to excuse myself and make a beeline for the buffet. About an hour later, however, Jeri was fast approaching me again, saying, "You didn't tell me that you were writing a book on bragging." With my tummy now satisfied, I was ready to help this accomplished woman overcome her bragging blocks and to build a better case for herself.

When I told her more about the concepts in this book, Jeri practically broke down in tears. She started to describe her humiliation at having multiple interviews, even being one of two finalists at several, and then never snagging the job. Rejection after rejection had undermined her confidence, and she worried that her determination was now coming across as desperation. "At first I thought it was nice that one guy called and apologized for not hiring me,

but now several others have done the same thing. I think
they feel sorry for me, and it stinks!" Then it hit her:
Maybe she was still jobless because she didn't know how
to promote herself. It was hard to disagree. "I was raised to
never talk about myself, and I still have a hard time with
it," Jeri said, explaining, "I'm the first person in my family to go to college, so I tend to be very self-conscious
about looking like a show-off."

I said, "Jeri, I've heard from everyone that you've done incredible things in your career, but I've got to be frank. When
I first asked you to tell me about yourself you were all over
the map and completely lost me. Can you just distill a few of
the highlights of your career?" Here is some of what she told
me (what I had to pull out of her is in parentheses):

"Most recently I worked for a nonprofit (as national
manager of communication!). I used to work in public affairs (as the director!), and then I decided to go back to
school (for a master's degree!)." She added, "I'm looking
for a new job, but no one wants to hire me." (I recommended, of course, that she quickly lose that last line!)

Realizing that she had her work cut out for her, we
agreed to get together a few days later for coffee to look at
her bragologue. This is what she finally came up with:

I started my career as a journalist, which eventually
landed me a position as public affairs director for one
of the boroughs, a job I held for eight years. I decided
from that experience to return to school for my master's in public administration. It wasn't easy, given that
I was raising my daughter as a single mom at the same
time, but now I am very proud to be the first person

in my family with not only a BA, but a master's degree as well! Following graduate school, I served in various positions with increasing responsibility for several leading nonprofit organizations, working my way up to a senior position for a national educational foundation. When my mother developed cancer I took a year off to help her, but now I am pursuing my next opportunity. Unfortunately I started looking just before 9/11, and now with the economy in a slump it hasn't been the best time to be job hunting. I know it's far harder lately than usual to find exactly the right thing, but with my background and persistence I am expecting something great to work out soon!

Ah, much better. And it didn't take a half-hour to explain! I know it's difficult to synopsize your life into a thirty-second brag bite or even a two-minute bragologue, but it's essential to create a *coherent summary* of where you have been, where you are at, and where you are going. Often your collection of experiences will necessitate more than one bragologue for a variety of occasions, depending on your audience and the message you want to send. Whatever the situation, you want to make it as easy as possible for people to get to know you and your story so they will keep you in mind when they hear of that perfect opportunity. When you tell a fuzzy or disjointed story, your audience loses interest and your bragging bombs.

SAY IT ANYHOW

"I don't know what to say about myself because I'm not sure what I want to do."

"I was really sick and so I had to quit my job as a book-

"But . . . when people brag it makes others feel bad."

Yes, it can have that effect if you are condescending or trying to one-up others. So be just as sensitive when you brag as you are with everything else in life.

keeper, and since then I haven't really been doing much of anything, except gardening. I'm well now, but I don't know what to do next and am really kind of worried about it all."

The speaker, an attractive forty-something woman named Robin, was responding to my question "So tell me what you've been up to lately" with this rather dreary assessment of her situation. Robin had come to me through a dear friend, and I had agreed to advise her on sorting out her next career move. Probing for details, I found out that she had spent nearly ten years working for a large plumbing-supply company as a bookkeeper, had an undergraduate degree in English from the University of Michigan, and was a single mom who was raising a teenage son. Yes, she'd had a mysterious illness for months, later determined to be a noncancerous brain tumor, which had been successfully removed. Now she was in the process of reassessing her life and deciding what to do next. One thing she was unsure about was whether to return to bookkeeping. "It's dry and boring, and to be honest, my boss drove me crazy for years. It's stressful, and stress is the last thing I need," she said. One thing was sure: Robin's bragologue was clearly in need of a pep talk.

I asked her what her passion in life was at the moment. She said, "Other than my son, I have to say it's my garden. At first, working in it was just therapeutic, a way of getting myself out in the sun and fresh air. But now I find that I have a green thumb." I asked her if this could possibly become her next career, and she said that she wasn't really sure, though the thought of perhaps working for a nursery had crossed her mind. Robin's biggest problem, however, continued to be her fear of saying anything of significance about herself to anyone, given her complete lack of clarity about what she wanted to do next with her life. And she wasn't actively working on making any plans, just hoping that maybe something would pop up.

I asked her if she had ever heard Yogi Berra's famous line, "When you come to a fork in the road, take it." She laughed, smiling for the first time in the conversation. I told Robin that it was time to throw away her old gloomologue. She needed to replace it by casting a wide net and by devising a proactive bragologue that bridged bookkeeping to gardening. Who knew what might result, but at least it was a start. She could use the new and improved Robin story to engage others in social situations, getting them interested in who she is and what she's about. Her bragologue turned into this:

> I was a bookkeeper for ten years and took time off to deal with some health problems, which fortunately have been resolved. Although I'm not sure what I want to do next, whether to go back to bookkeeping or consider other possibilities, it's been great having this time off. I've been able to really throw myself more than ever into my true passion, which is gardening. I'm even thinking about ideas for combining my love of plants with a new career.

A pretty simple fix, huh? Sometimes the best way out of a "what should I do next" quandary is to begin by just saying *something.* Often when our thoughts become words, our words become deeds. The more you say something, the more you start to believe it, and the more likely it is to become a reality. And what did Robin end up doing next? She was hired to work for a family-owned landscape design company, but not to do the books. She's the operations manager and second in command.

ALWAYS A WORK IN PROGRESS

"I may be retired, but don't count me out!"
     The days of withdrawing to the sidelines and watching the parade go by from your rocking chair or golf cart when you hit your sixties are fading. With people main-

taining their health and vitality well into their senior years, many who retire find themselves beating back the boredom blues by going on to second careers or working part time. Even if you've relinquished your career or an impressive job title, don't be so quick to toss out your brag bag. You never know when you might want to do a little—or a lot of—work again.

June, who was in her seventies, had a three-decade career in the incentive travel industry and had recently retired to enjoy time with her grandchildren, remodel her home, and "finally catch up on all the things I wanted to catch up on for the last thirty years." Initially she thought her working days were over. But less than eighteen months into her retirement, a company where she had once been employed ten years before contacted her about doing some consulting work to help restructure their in-house incentive travel department. In early contacts with the firm, she was ambivalent about getting involved and initially played down her value to them. When Hank, the company president, first contacted her, she said that she was enjoying her retirement and not sure if an "old granny" like herself had the energy to keep up. Besides, weren't some of the people who were already working at the firm as qualified for the role as she was?

Hank wasn't put off so easily, and June soon realized that she might enjoy this part-time assignment after all. "I remodeled the kitchen. We traveled for a while. I got caught up on all those things I never used to get to, and then life felt a little humdrum. Full retirement is not what I thought it would be," she said. But in further talks with the firm, she discovered that they were expecting to be able to compensate her far below the going rate. Now that she was interested, she had to dig herself out of the hole she had put herself in by being so self-deprecating in the previous conversations, and make sure that she was not only given the consulting position but also paid appropriately. Once she decided to pursue the job, June switched gears and developed a persuasive bragologue to present her accomplishments and qualifications in a more compelling way. She wrote the president this e-mail:

Hank, my true value to the company far exceeds my experience in simply arranging travel. I have a reputation with those in the field based on thirty-plus years in the industry, during which time I've consistently been in tune with the needs of the sales force. In addition, as you know, I served for many years on the board of our international trade organization and have contacts worldwide. I am certain my expertise will enable you to not only successfully restructure, but also help you to stretch the dollars in your program budget. Given the value of my reputation, my experience, and my connections, I anticipate being compensated for my services at an industry-standard rate. Besides, I am truly enjoying my retirement, and you are going to need to entice me out of it!

June landed the consulting position and at the rate she wanted. From that time on, she never let her bragologues get sloppy again. Remember, even if you think you're calling it quits you might be back in the game sooner than anticipated, so keep your bragologues current and crisp.

BRAG ANYWAY

"The truth is, I'm not doing anything that would impress any-one."

I met Lonnie when we were thrown together as co-chairwomen of a committee for a women's trade group in San Francisco. For our first meeting, she invited me to lunch at a private club atop one of the city's most beautiful skyscrapers. While the view was dazzling and the decor impeccable, I was even more impressed with Lonnie. She had a genuine ease about her, gliding through the room, talking with other members seated at the tables. As we ate, she told me the story of her career rise. She knew all the power brokers in the financial community. After our stint as co-chairs, our paths diverged for the next year or so as we plunged back into our routines. About five months ago, wanting to check in with her and see how she was doing, I sent an e-mail to her office. It bounced back. When I called, the number had been disconnected. I started asking around, but no one seemed to know where she had gone. Hmm, curious.

Two weeks later I was racing through my local Barnes & Noble on a weekday afternoon, when I spotted a Lonnie lookalike. The woman was wearing old blue jeans and sneakers while drinking coffee and flipping through a book, a far cry from the Lonnie I knew, always decked out in an elegant power suit, rushing madly but purposefully from meeting to meeting. Maybe Lonnie had a twin. I inched a little closer to get a better look and then called out her name. She looked up and we squealed with delight at having discovered one another in this unlikely place. As we spent the next hour catching up, she explained why I hadn't been able to reach her at her work number. "Last November I was sitting in a meeting with my boss discussing our strategy for the upcoming year when something very strange came over me. I don't know what triggered it," she said, adding, "I was pretty happy with my life, although I was always looking for ways to have more balance. Suddenly I had the most incredible sense of clar-

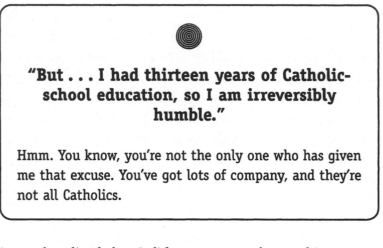

"But . . . I had thirteen years of Catholic-school education, so I am irreversibly humble."

Hmm. You know, you're not the only one who has given me that excuse. You've got lots of company, and they're not all Catholics.

ity and realized that I did not want to be working at my job anymore. I was done. I wanted out."

She didn't tell her boss right away, waiting a few weeks to see if her feelings would change. They didn't, even after she bounced the idea off some of her more cautious and conservative friends, who asked, "Are you crazy? Leaving at the height of your career in your mid-forties? In the middle of a recession? Bad idea." Despite the warnings, Lonnie announced her resignation, much to the surprise of her bank colleagues, and has been without a job for over nine months. Although she is increasingly anxious about her situation, she finds herself saying no to the various and sundry headhunters who call trying to lure her back to the old life. So when I asked her, "What are you doing now?" she stammered, replying, "Nothing that would impress you, I am sorry to say." She continued on about how she had the hardest time answering that question, telling me that as a banker she used to have her story down pat, knowing exactly what she did and what she could do for others. It was easy to talk about. But since quitting, she had spent her time doing nothing particularly exciting to the outside world and found the whole process of explaining herself rather challenging, if not exhausting.

I told her that her current story, in fact, revealed something quite positive: courage. Although the whole notion of dropping out has lost some of its stigma as the workplace has become more humanized thanks to women, most people only dream of doing what she had done. Further, I loved hearing her tell me about the supposedly mundane activities she had been up to. Knowing about them gave me a much deeper sense of who Lonnie really is as a person outside of her expertise in the financial world. I told her that, as she slowly moved back into the world of networking, she needed to create a bragologue.

A few days later Lonnie and I met again, this time for dinner. She said, "Peggy, ask me again: 'What are you doing now?' " When I did she surprised me with her new bragologue, which went something like this:

If anyone had told me this time last year that I would no longer be a banker, and not working in the job I had done for twenty years, I would have said they were nuts. But that's exactly what happened. Everything was going well in my career—high-end clients, a great boss, fabulous bonuses—but about a year ago, I woke up one day and realized that this part of my life was done. It was so strange because I've always been so practical and directed. I went to college, got my MBA, entered the financial world with gusto, worked like crazy, and climbed my way up the ladder. I couldn't think of doing anything else. Until, however, I experienced a real gut feeling that I was ready to move on. I tinkered with the idea for a while, although at the time I wasn't sure what I wanted, just that I knew I didn't want to do my job any longer. So I resigned! This past year I've been doing all the things I've wanted to do but couldn't because of my eighty-hour workweeks. And you know, even on days when I think, "What have I done?" I know I did the right thing and I am grateful that I've been able to take this time off. I've gone rock climbing, re-landscaped my garden, painted my entire downstairs, taught myself how to reupholster a couch, audited two art history courses, and had lots of meetings with headhunters. I have finally narrowed the field of choice for my next career, and I know I want it to be related to women's issues, in either the for-profit or nonprofit sector. Right now I'm looking at CEO, COO, or director-of-development positions.

Of course, this was Lonnie's full-blown base bragologue. She was planning to adjust it according to whom she was talking to, pulling out bits and pieces here and there, depending on the situation. When she was finished with her bragologue, she looked at me straight in the eye, took a deep breath, and said, "God, I feel better already. I don't feel like such a shlump!"

GO BEYOND JUST THE KIDS

"I had a hard time getting her past the cupcakes."

There is not a job on this planet that is harder, demands more talent, or is more important than raising kids. Although only an aunt, both by blood and as a surrogate, I've watched and helped as my sisters and friends have raised their kids into extraordinary human beings. And yet many of those who leave the workforce to raise a family often feel like second-class citizens, especially at cocktail parties when people are tooting about their seemingly more exciting endeavors. The cute thing that Johnny said at breakfast or the trip to the emergency room to extract the Cheerio stuck up his nose seems to pale in comparison to an enviable new job, the company's business win, or the partner's latest African safari. So what are the bragging basics for today's "domestic engineers," especially those who plan on entering the workforce again? Well, you need to go beyond Johnny and talk about yourself: your background, any plans that you have, what you are learning from your stay-at-home position, or other things you might be involved in (community service, hobbies) that make you interesting and memorable. Create a bragologue reflecting what's so good about your past, present, and future that has less to do with your children and more to do with you.

Wendy, a high-level client of mine, came to me recently with a problem. One of her firm's most important customers, Robert, had asked for a favor. His wife had taken time off to care for the children, but was looking for a part-time paid position in the nonprofit world now that her youngest had started school. Robert asked Wendy if she would sit with his wife, Cheryl, at an upcoming corporate dinner they were all going to be attending next month and discuss her qualifications. He was hoping Wendy could recommend her to a few of her contacts in the foundation world. She agreed to talk with Cheryl, and just before the dinner, Robert sent her a recent newspaper article about his wife's involvement with a group who put together a hospital reading program for children with chronic illnesses.

The evening of the dinner, Wendy made sure she was seated next to Cheryl, who started the conversation by talking about her day baking cupcakes for her son's class. She was very proud that, although she was far from being an expert baker, she had done everything from scratch, using only healthy ingredients. Wendy heard about the cupcakes in excruciating detail: how Cheryl had bought organic flour, used pink dye made from beets for the frosting, and decorated the goodies with all-natural miniature marshmallows, which were better than those hard red candies that the little ones might choke on. When Wendy asked her about herself, Cheryl's response was the equivalent of a footnote: "I grew up in the South, went to a small women's college in North Carolina, then worked in merchandising in the handbag department of a large department store in Dallas. Before my kids were born, I did some volunteer work with the local hospitals." It was all so understated that Wendy began to wonder whether she had misheard her client's request. Cheryl didn't sound like someone who wanted a job.

Sensing it had been a long time since Cheryl felt there was anything to brag about in terms of her "outside" activities, Wendy pressed on: "So I hear you'd like to start doing some work with foundations. I read about how successful you were at raising money for the reading program. Can you tell me more about the fundraising work you've done?" With a little probing, it all came pouring out: Cheryl's volunteer work turned out to be quite substantial. Apparently she had quite a knack for soliciting money, and had done so very successfully for several organizations. Beyond the reading program, she had helped raise $15 million for the hospital's new pediatric wing through individual donors and several fundraising events she had chaired. Cheryl had turned around a local charity for teens on the brink of closing by taking over as board president and writing grant proposals. Her most recent project had been helping her college roommate, now living in rural Maine, raise money for a health clinic. Although Cheryl seemed perfectly able to mentor a friend on foundation grant writing or approach a private donor to ask for millions, she was hard-pressed to tell someone at a cocktail party about her own accomplishments.

When people, especially women, choose to leave the

workforce and become stay-at-home parents, they tell me that they fear losing their identities. Yes, little-Johnny stories are great if you are in the company of others with similar interests and if that's not all you talk about. But even parents tell me that they get bored with nonstop kiddie talk. So in order to avoid the second-class-citizen treatment in broader social situations, come prepared with bragologues about yourself, not just your kids!

CHAPTER 8

When You're Out on Your Own

- "He introduced me the wrong way. I was horrified."
- "My website is ready, and I'm all set for business."
- "It was a stretch even for me."
- "I've always remembered what she said when we met."
- "He was all flash."

When you *are* the company, promoting yourself takes on a whole new meaning. In effect, you have to become a walking billboard for your business (without sounding like one!). Whether you're a graphic artist, an accountant, a freelance writer, a management consultant, or a software developer, it's really all the same: You've got to brag every chance you get, and that means being ready 24/7. Your livelihood and future, along with all the sweat equity and dollars invested, depend on how good you become at self-promotion, at telling your story in a catchy manner and distinguishing yourself so that you rise above the fray. The bottom line is quite simple: *Before you sell anything, you've got to first sell yourself in a personal and memorable way.*

Most new business owners that I have met and coached,

however, fall victim to brag-fright. While they can go on and on about their products or services, even the most skilled and polished professionals fumble when I ask them to shine the spotlight on themselves—to speak about what they've accomplished and how it connects to the services or products they are selling. They are at a loss for words when it comes to articulating the very things about themselves that will differentiate them from the competition, demonstrate their effectiveness, bolster credibility, instill confidence, and personalize their pitch into a message that resonates. They let unchecked brag-fright get in the way of developing the self-promotion approach needed to stand out from the competition and make the deal.

"But . . . it's okay to brag about someone else, just not about myself."

That's a shame, because what you're really saying is that you're not as proud of yourself as you are of others or that you aren't as accomplished as others. If this sounds familiar, then you've got some work ahead!

Further, talk to most entrepreneurs about promotion, and all they see are the dollar signs connected with an advertising campaign, event sponsorship, hiring a fancy publicist, or developing reams of collateral materials. But effective promotion of your business has less to do with the amount of dollars spent on expensive marketing campaigns and everything to do with how well you personally communicate your story on a daily basis wherever you go. And I don't mean repeating what's written on your website or brochure. Take the time to carefully craft personal and conversational bragologues and brag bites customized to meet a wide variety of situations, both planned and impromptu. Be ready to pitch a prospective client or venture capitalist, talk to a journalist, or spread the word about your company to family, friends, or the guy mowing his lawn down the street! It's one of the surest ways to maximize your exposure without spending a dime.

MAKE SURE YOUR FANS GET IT RIGHT

"He introduced me the wrong way. I was horrified."

As any entrepreneur knows, friends and family members can be an important source for contacts and for spreading the word to the outside world about the rising success of your business. But sometimes you need to literally put the right words in their mouths so they will convey the correct message about who you are, what you're doing, and your successes or goals. One budding entrepreneur I recently coached learned this lesson in a painful and embarrassing way.

After twelve years Judy had tossed away the New York City rat race and her impressive advertising career for an idyllic country lifestyle in a small New England town. In the advertising world she had risen to the rank of account director, but now she longed to return to her roots as a writer. In fact, she had a degree in journalism and had started her career as a promotional copywriter for a well-established women's magazine on Madison Avenue. Longer term, she envisioned becoming an author. But in the short run, to prove herself and to make ends meet, she was ready to try her hand at any type of writing. Enchanted with her new countrified lifestyle, and anxious to meet other professionals in her area, she took on some local assignments. She wrote a brochure for a local real estate agency, a quarterly newsletter on fabric care for a large regional dry cleaner, and ad copy for a restaurant.

Judy told me that after about six months, "Phase One," as she called it, had ended, adding, "I was so overqualified and underpaid, it was ridiculous. Now it was time for the big stuff and Phase Two." She called all her city contacts in advertising, spreading the word that she was available as a freelance copywriter. Before she knew it she was landing some great work. She was quickly hired to write the copy for a major TV ad campaign and for a promotional video that ran in one of the largest U.S. retail chains, among other assignments. With her portfolio of work expanding and her confidence growing, she was anxious to begin planting seeds for Phase Three, fulfilling her dream of becoming an author. She had a few nonfiction book ideas, and wanted to make herself available for ghostwriting projects as well. The perfect networking opportunity presented itself by way of an engagement party that she threw for her sister and future brother-in-law, Brian, where some of the invited guests of the couple were heavyweights in the New York publishing world.

Judy was especially interested in meeting one guest in particular, a book editor who was an old friend of Brian's from childhood. When the big moment came, Brian said to the editor, "I'd like to introduce you to my future sister-in-law, Judy, who is throwing this beautiful party today. She's a New York City transplant who has struck out on her own as a freelance writer and has written for . . ." Suddenly Brian paused, looking to Judy to complete his sentence. Before Judy knew it, Brian continued, saying, "She's been doing some great things. She wrote a newsletter for one of the largest dry cleaners in this area and has been working with a hot new restaurant. Wasn't that newsletter you did on fabric care?" Judy was mortified and felt her face flush. How was she ever going to brag her way from writing copy for a local dry cleaner to writing a best-selling book? She smiled uneasily, and responded, "Hi. It's nice to meet you. Well, I actually have been doing some work that I'm pretty excited about . . ." but before she had a chance to elaborate, the editor's wife called him away and they left soon after. That was it, an opportunity lost.

The next day, she lightly chastised her misinformed future brother-in-law. Bringing him up to speed on her Phase Two accomplishments and Phase Three goals, she begged him to never mention the dry cleaner ever again!

I can't stress enough the importance of making sure that people who are going to introduce you have the facts right about your current situation and goals. We often think we don't have much control over what others say, but we do. When others introduce you, they often either repeat what they have heard from you or make something up. So get your bragologues and brag bites down, repeat them often, and make sure to keep them current so that others have the most up-to-date version.

Apply similar techniques in prepping the person who will be introducing you when you are making a speech. I recently got a call from a friend complaining about the lame setup she got as the keynote speaker to a group of four hundred professors at a university. Not only did the person forget to mention her twenty-three-year career as a journalist, but also that she had taught for this same university early in her career, and that she was now returning to the academic field. Instead, she was introduced as the person who wrote some obscure website, a writing job she had taken as she was transitioning from one career to another. It wasn't as bad as the dry cleaner, but it was close!

Having been zinged a few times myself before a speech, I now always call ahead to the person making the introduction and say, "I just want to get a feel for how you will be introducing me, so I can segue into my presentation." Nine times out of ten, I hear "Well, I was kind of thinking about . . ." or "I hadn't thought about it. Do you have any suggestions?" I then give them my bragologue, customized to the occasion, of course. This not only ensures that I am presented in the most current and appropriate light, but the person making the introduction often appreciates my thoughtfulness. She's usually frazzled about getting up to speak herself, so it's one less thing for her to worry about. Remember: A successful word-of-mouth bragging campaign is contingent upon getting the words right to begin with!

DON'T OVERLOOK
THE MOST IMPORTANT ELEMENT

"My website is ready, and I'm all set for business."

Tim, a thirty-year-old computer guru, boy wonder, and the son of my neighbor, left his job in corporate America a year ago to develop a simple piece of software that he is convinced will revolutionize online collaboration. With the software complete, he has officially formed his company and brought in two college friends. Initially the plan is to sell the software directly off the company's website and to get the word out through the press and by networking at trade shows. Tim, who sits at the helm, has followed all the rules for presenting a professional image of the company: He designed a flashy website and logo, printed a four-color brochure, purchased the finest and most expensive business cards with matching stationery and envelopes, and even invested in giveaway pens and mugs that are imprinted with his company's name and catchy logo. He's all set for business and raring to go.

Nine months into his venture, I ran into Tim and asked how things were going. He said, "Pretty good, though the market is tough." I told him that my company was looking to buy collaboration tools, and to stop by and show me what he had. We made an appointment and when he arrived, Tim laid out his materials on the table, including his freebie pens and mugs. All of it had the markings of a well-conceived, marketing-oriented start-up until Tim opened his mouth:

As you know, Peggy, I have developed what I believe
is the most revolutionary software in the collaboration space that brings about a significant paradigm
shift in powerful, scalable, end-to-end development
solutions. [I would later learn that this was the lead-
in on the company's press release. No wonder the
press wasn't returning his calls.] It is based on peer-
to-peer computing. Let me explain. It's where com-
puters bypass third-party web-based servers and
connect directly point-to-point. The technology is
Internet-based versus web-based. Most people think
they are one and the same, but they aren't. The World
Wide Web is not the Internet. It's just a small piece of
the larger picture, which is the Internet. If you have
heard about peer-to-peer computing, you're probably
thinking of Napster, but our product has nothing to
do with Napster. In fact, most companies that sell
peer-to-peer products are . . .

He continued with his encyclopedic technical knowledge
of the market. Eventually he got to his product and in
painstaking detail provided a demonstration. Unfortunately, by that time my eyes were glazed over and all I
wanted was to get him out of the office. By the time he
finished, I was nearly comatose and it was going to take
several cups of coffee in his logoed mug to revive me!

Tim had broken every rule of effective self-promotion,
and no fancy website, logo, brochure, or freebie pen was
going to save him. He hadn't taken the time to develop a
short, pithy bragologue, so his whole pitch sounded more
like a product blabologue. To make matters even worse, he

was suffering from one of the worst cases of geek-speak I had ever encountered.

Everything I needed to know would have easily come out, had he just bothered to answer a few simple questions:

1. What's your background? How did this product come to be? (Presumably, once he told me, I would have confidence in what he was selling.)
2. How will your product benefit my business? (He hadn't taken the time to ask me about my company and its needs. I didn't care if the software let me work on complicated 3D models. I wanted to know whether I could use it for laying out my brochures, sales presentations, workshop booklets, or sharing photos with my freelance staff across the country.)
3. Is it easy to use? (Very important to a non–technically oriented company.)
4. Can I afford it? (A deal breaker or maker!)

After bringing myself back to consciousness I was honest with Tim, telling him he had failed to make the sale and why. I offered him a second chance. He returned a few days later with answers to the above questions and a cut-off time of fifteen minutes max. Here is what Tim said on the second go-round:

1. What's your background? How did this product come to be?

After graduating from UCLA with a degree in mechanical engineering, I worked for ten years designing high-end surgical devices that many hospitals are still using. I worked my way up and became director of new product development, responsible for overseeing more than fifteen product teams working on the design and development of twenty new devices annually. More and more as the company grew, the team designing a particular device was geographically dispersed. For example, one person would be in New York, another in Europe, and yet another in California. I was looking for a way for the teams to collaborate on our projects in real time over the Internet, so that we could work more efficiently, avoid miscommunication, and lessen travel time and costs for team meetings.

This became even more important after 9/11, given that many employees were fearful of flying and everyone wanted to stay closer to home. Having three young children myself, I could really understand their feelings. I researched the market, experimented with a few products and services, and found that there weren't any reliable and cost-effective solutions that would allow me to collaborate on any type of data or documents, from simple Word documents and PowerPoint presentations to more complicated 3D models. So I decided to develop a powerful, fast, and easy-to-use software that could handle the job and be used by anyone in virtually any industry.

2. How will your product benefit my business?

As the founder and CEO of a small, growing company myself, I know how important it is to stretch your dollar as far as it can go and streamline operations as much as possible. When you are on your own and getting started, you wear many different hats, and time to get it all done is in short supply. So our software has been designed with you in mind. For example, Peggy, you were telling me earlier that you're currently working with your graphic designer on a twenty-page workshop booklet while you've been on the road. With our software, instead of your designer in Berkeley e-mailing the specs to you, then you marking changes to e-mail back and trying to explain what you really meant by them, you and the designer would just get on the phone, click a button, and both be looking at the exact same design at the same time. When you annotate or mark up the design, she can see it instantly on her computer screen and vice versa. All the back-and-forth of e-mailing, faxing, sending overnight packages is eliminated, as well as the costs, time delays, frustration, and potential for miscommunication.

Say no more, Tim. I got it. Now I see the advantage. You sold me! Tim hadn't made just a product sale, he had made a *personal* sale. Remember that effective self-promotion isn't about going on and on about yourself for no reason. When it comes to selling your products and services, first get to know your customers, and then be prepared to brag about yourself and who you are in a storylike way that portrays your strong points, tying into the interests and unique needs of your customers.

BELIEVE IN YOURSELF OR NO ONE ELSE WILL

"It was a stretch even for me."

How do you stretch yourself from being a prize-winning landscape architect to a popular author and publisher?

"I needed a bragologue that was going to leap tall buildings in a single bound," said Gail, reflecting on her road to success, adding, "and part of it was conveying pure passion and belief in what I was doing even though I knew nothing about publishing."

Gail had spent thirteen years running her own landscape design firm, working on all sorts of private and public outdoor spaces, from homes and businesses to parks, golf courses, and country clubs. With the arrival of her first child, she was looking to transition into something that allowed her to stay closer to home and afforded more flexible hours.

One day at a gathering of her mothers' group, one woman remarked, "You know, someone should write a book about places to get married around here. When I was planning my wedding, there wasn't a single resource book out there to help me put it all together."

It was a light-bulb moment for Gail. She recalled having had a similarly frustrating experience three years prior when she got married. Eureka! She would publish the first guidebook for brides about places available to hold weddings and parties in her sprawling metropolitan backyard and outlying areas. She was practically exploding with excitement by the time she left the meeting. Her fate was sealed; her new venture, a fait accompli.

The fact that she knew nothing about publishing or

event planning did little to deter her. (Look up the word *determined* in the dictionary and you'll see Gail's picture right beside it!) Off she went, researching the bridal and event-planning industry from top to bottom, arming herself with statistics to later convince establishments to advertise in her guidebook. She set about writing a few sample chapters and designing a cover, which she would later need to showcase her concept to bookstores, distributors, gift and bridal shops, and office supply stores. She knew that advertisers would never commit their promotional dollars up front unless she could guarantee wide distribution.

When she went out on sales calls here is what she said:

I have been living in the Bay Area for over twenty years, and am a graduate of UC Berkeley with an undergraduate degree in environmental engineering and a master's in business administration. For the last ten years, I have been a successful business owner. Until recently I was a landscape architect designing a variety of private and public spaces. It wasn't a walk in the park that gave me this idea, however, but a walk down the aisle. When I planned for my wedding, there wasn't a single resource guidebook out there to help me put it all together. Here I was with twenty thousand dollars ready to invest in my big day—the average cost of a wedding these days—but I didn't know where to spend it! There were snippets of information here and there, but nothing that provided a single-source, comprehensive list of facilities available, costs, amenities, as well as all the other services,

from catering to flowers. And you know, the same
type of information was lacking for businesses planning parties. Not a single resource! Having designed
the landscapes of everything from country clubs to
restaurants, I can tell you that there is a wealth of facilities. My book will hit two birds with one stone.

Once Gail talked one bookstore chain into agreeing to
carry the guide, the first facility signed an advertising con-
tract, and from there the domino effect took over. (Of
course, she always bragged to prospective clients about
who had signed on, highlighting the bigwigs.) After the
first edition came out, her phone started ringing off the
hook and businesses were begging to become paid advertisers in her book. Looking back, Gail admits, "I was
frightened at first, but I gathered my strength and simply
acted as if the business was already up and running successfully." Her can-do attitude, a bragologue that leaped
tall buildings in a single bound, an enormous amount of
enthusiasm, and the belief that she could do it served to
make success a reality.

"But . . . isn't bragging just showing off?"

If you weave your accomplishments artfully and enter-
tainingly into the conversation, no one will think you're
a show-off. In fact, they'll ask to hear more.

Today, twelve years later, Gail has a highly successful hybrid business in publishing, advertising, and marketing consulting. Her book is now in its ninth printing, with versions for Los Angeles and Hawaii, and last year she started an events trade magazine.

MAKE YOUR BRAG BITES STICK

"Even after six months, I remembered what she said when we met."

When I started my company seven years ago, like many aspiring entrepreneurs I attended my share of local networking events. More often than not, they turned out to be a feeding frenzy of professionals pitching me all sorts of products and services as a new small-business owner. While at first I loved the attention, after a few of these events the flattery began to wear thin. Everyone was beginning to look and sound the same. If you had heard one, you had heard them all, until I met Fran. She was an easygoing and likeable thirty-something business development specialist going solo with her own consulting company. At first, I braced myself for the typical "As a business development specialist, I offer a variety of experience and skills in administration, finance, information services, marketing, sales, training, and operations." Instead, Fran surprised me with this clever little brag bite: "You know how people think puppies are so cute and they can't resist taking care of them? Well, that's how I feel about baby businesses. I love helping them grow and watching them prosper." She went on to tell me about several businesses she had gotten off the ground, all the while asking me about mine. Fran not only had a gracious and genuine ease to her, she had a catchy way of summing up what she did. Six months later, when my business was bursting at the seams, I went searching for her card.

When I stress the importance of saying something interesting about yourself and your accomplishments, many people make the mistake of thinking that means I want them to come up with a clever advertising slogan. But the problem with slogans is that they often sound like a cliché or come off as too cutesy. When I say Become a walking billboard, I mean that you always need to be out there promoting yourself. But brag catchy, not corny. Think of ways to tell your story that are humorous or even metaphorical, and make sure to be original and authentic.

BACK UP STYLE WITH SUBSTANCE

"He was all flash."

Recently, I had the pleasure of coaching Roland, the CEO and founder of a multimillion-dollar property management conglomerate, for an upcoming presentation. When I told Roland about the book I was writing on bragging, he remarked, "Boy, do I have some stories for you." One in particular concerned a young man in his mid-twenties named Dru, who had recently paid him a visit trying to drum up interest and capital for a new business he was starting. Roland agreed to meet with Dru as a favor to the young man's father, whom Roland had worked with for years. As Roland said, "His son was considering starting a company in the construction trade. He wanted me to meet with him to give him some feedback since I had spent my life in the industry. Of course, in a veiled kind of way, he was dangling a carrot and looking for early investors."

The day of the meeting at Roland's home, Dru showed up impeccably groomed, dressed to the hilt in a fine Armani suit, with a bronzed glow on his face in the dead of winter. He was the total image of success. As the two walked to the meeting room, Dru asked Roland excitedly, "Is that your black Mercedes in the driveway?" Upon hearing that it was, Dru mentioned that he owned the same car, pointing out the window to his brand-new shiny red Mercedes SLK-500, mentioning how he preferred it to the Lexus he had previously owned. He then asked Roland if he was a golfer, mentioning how he had passed a club a few miles down the road. Roland replied that he was, and Dru stated that he too belonged to a certain golf club, well known for its outrageous membership fees. Roland was slightly put off, noting, "He kind of went out of his way to make these points. I felt like all he could brag about was expensive material stuff."

The two sat down in Roland's study, and Dru immediately launched into his business concept. Roland thought the concept, while interesting, would take a lot of muscle and business savvy to get off the ground. Wondering whether Dru was up to the task, he inquired about his history, naturally expecting to hear about the business success that had landed him that shiny Mercedes.

Dru described his past with brag bites right and left that unfortunately missed the mark and had little to do with developing a business. After attending a prestigious New

England prep school, he had attended a small and exclusive liberal arts college in Ohio and graduated with a degree in art history. For the next two years he had worked for his father's company in the back office, structuring some vague financial deals. He had also tried his hand at project management for a large construction company in Texas, but left after a year, admitting sheepishly that he didn't like the weather. He eventually decided to get his MBA, and had graduated from an Ivy League school, his father's alma mater. Dru had plenty of business smarts as the son of a successful business owner in the oil and gas industry. Graduate school had also prepared him well. His senior thesis had been a case history of one of the largest construction companies in the world, which is really how he came up with his new-business idea in the first place. He also had a strong background in financial management. Trying to impress Roland, he threw out some newfangled investment ideas he had learned in class, and that he had been successfully applying to his trust fund.

As Roland said to me later, laughing, "Remember that famous Wendy's commercial with the little old lady asking, 'Where's the beef?' That's exactly what I wanted to say." It was clear to Roland that Dru had never really gotten his hands dirty and had yet to experience material worry of any sort. "Imagine," said Roland, "investing in some slick Willie who might spend your money like it's going out of style?"

If Dru had done his homework and read up on Roland, he might have taken a different approach. Roland had come from a lower-middle-class family and had built his company from scratch. In fact, his is the classic story: Boy starts in the mailroom of a Fortune 500 company and ends up saving enough money to start his own company at thirty, now worth $100 million. Oh, and the Mercedes parked in the driveway? It was a gift from his wife for his

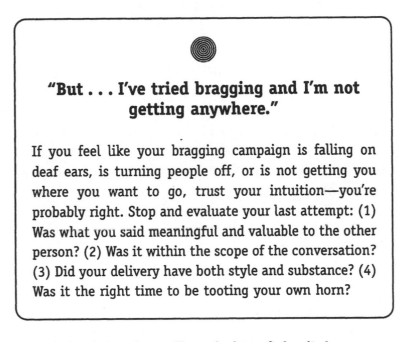

"But . . . I've tried bragging and I'm not getting anywhere."

If you feel like your bragging campaign is falling on deaf ears, is turning people off, or is not getting you where you want to go, trust your intuition—you're probably right. Stop and evaluate your last attempt: (1) Was what you said meaningful and valuable to the other person? (2) Was it within the scope of the conversation? (3) Did your delivery have both style and substance? (4) Was it the right time to be tooting your own horn?

sixtieth birthday that still made him feel a little uncomfortable every time he drove it.

We've all heard the advice "Dress for success" or "Dress the part." That's fine, but make sure you back up style with real substance. Style without substance often feels like a charade (and most people can spot imposters within minutes). On the other hand, substance without style will put an insomniac to sleep. You need to seek a balance. Dru thought his successful look, his material possessions, his fancy schooling and degrees would carry the day. It was the unspoken cornerstone of his bragging campaign, and it bombed royally. That's because good bragging is invisible; it works its way seamlessly, and it's loaded with genuine pride and enthusiasm. As Dru needed to learn, that's the only way to brag and get away with it.

CHAPTER 9

———————◎———————

Brag Nags

I warn you. Skip this chapter at your own risk.
—Peggy Klaus, brag nag

You've answered "Take 12"; your brag bag is filled. You've read through multiple scenarios from a wide variety of situations, highlighting bragging bests and bragging bombs. Now you're feeling pumped and ready to get out there and, well, *brag!* For the first time in your life, tooting your own horn might even be kind of fun. But *stop.* Before you get started, there are just a few more things I need to tell you about—call them my brag nags—elements of your delivery that you absolutely must get right to be a successful bragger.

Brag Nag #1:
BORE NO MORE

After hearing a boring braggart go on and on, you probably never said to yourself, "Gee, I wish he had talked longer!" Yet when we step into the spotlight, we often turn into that drone everyone dreads having to listen to. Where did we pick up such bad behavior? Most likely in what I call Presentation Training 101, the public-speaking courses and workshops that are the closest most of us get to a formal education in how to talk about ourselves. Many of us receive this instruction in college or at corporate workshops, especially if we are in sales and marketing. We assume these programs will serve us well—after all, *experts* teach them—but the surprising truth is, many lead to more harm than good. And if you believe that Presentation Training 101 is the be-all and end-all of self-promotion, to be applied right down to your brag bites and bragologues, you'll get yourself into even deeper trouble. You're not only likely to be dull and uninspiring when you toot, but the kind of bragger who makes people want to run to the nearest exit.

Given that Presentation Training 101 courses and workshops are well meaning, how do they turn otherwise personable professionals into automatons? They tend to preach burdensome and rigid formulas: Tell 'em what you're going to tell 'em, tell 'em, and then wrap it up by telling 'em what you've just told 'em. Don't ever cross your arms in front of your chest. Never put your hands in your pockets, on your hips, in front of your crotch, or behind your back. Don't step out of an imagined golden triangle on the floor, to name just a few.

Worse yet, Presentation Training 101 is typically based on an old-school, stodgy way of speaking. Favoring formality over a conversational style, it actually discourages us from finding and talking in our own voice. Because the focus is often so much on formula and facts, we rarely learn to develop an engaging personal communication style. Knowing how to deliver brags bites and bragologues in a natural, conversational delivery separates powerful speakers from weak ones and effective braggers from intolerable ones.

The old-school approach also tends to overlook what's at the core of effective communication across the board: being your authentic best self. People connect more positively to you when you summon the power of your unique personality. So dump that facade and forget about others' expectations of what you should be or act like. When you genuinely engage your best self, when you combine warmth with strength and marry style with substance, others instantly perceive you from a fresh perspective and actually look forward to hearing what you have to say next.

Brag Nag #2:
BRING YOUR BEST SELF FORWARD

When I first started coaching business people, after years in the entertainment industry, I was stunned to discover how many of them check their personalities at the door, failing to bring their best self to the workplace. This was especially true with new hires and young workers and with people meeting colleagues or customers for the first time. One Wall Street client remarked after six months at his new job with an investment bank, "When I walk into the building at seven a.m., I become a completely different person. It's like I'm Mr. Hyde instead of Dr. Jekyll. I put on a mask and hide behind it. I become someone else entirely until I walk out the door at seven p.m."

While workers tend to loosen up over time, many still cling to a kind of mythic professional persona under the banner of the "corporate citizen." This translates into an aloof, unanimated, and unemotional style, or what I often refer to as the Joe Friday School of Communication. Named for the television detective from *Dragnet* who cautioned his witnesses to give him "just the facts, ma'am," this school breeds professionals who are so worried about the facts, they don't remember "I'm human. I'm funny. I'm a good listener. I'm friendly." They think only about what they're saying and forget to pay attention to how they are saying it.

Taking a Second Look at Professionalism

A few years ago, I worked with one young insurance executive who confided that his family and all his friends outside of work considered him to be an extremely funny, extroverted, and talkative guy. Mr. Congeniality! Unfortunately, his office mates didn't think so. In fact, on more than one occasion his boss had told him to lighten up. My client, however, thought he wouldn't be considered professional unless he behaved in a "serious" manner and always stuck to discussing the business at hand. I explained to him that simply being "serious" doesn't connote knowledge or command respect, or necessarily move projects along any faster. In fact, acting somber all the time is a significant turnoff for people who want to enjoy themselves while they work hard. Once my client became convinced that bringing his other self to the office was worth a try, he quickly developed a more informal style that was full of his quick wit and subtle humor. He was surprised at the avalanche of positive feedback he received from both colleagues and clients.

Many people fail to reinforce the qualities that work so well for them in their personal lives—friendliness, warmth, humor, energy, justified pride, sincerity, interest, and enthusiasm—which are what create rapport with others and draw people to them. These characteristics, when combined with substance, are essential to making a memorable impression and laying the groundwork for effective bragging. Lacking these traits, Joe Friday communicators come off as stiff, boring, unapproachable, and at times, even suspect.

Massaging Personality Traits

When I say authentic best self, I mean the parts of your personality that come out when you are surrounded by friends and loved ones who appreciate you and make you feel comfortable. One client, who headed a department of more than twenty people, was so shy around the office that he sat at his desk with his telephone headset on, even when he wasn't on the phone. When I questioned him about his behavior, he first claimed that not wanting to put the headset on and take it off all day was "an efficiency thing." After more probing, he admitted there was some truth to the observation of others that keeping the headset on was a way to ensure that people wouldn't approach him. After reflecting on the negative impact his headset habit was having on his co-workers and his superiors—who increasingly viewed him as arrogant and aloof because he avoided cubicle chitchat—he began to step out of his shell and reveal small details about himself to others. As he interacted more with his colleagues, soon even this extreme introvert was able to talk fearlessly and at length about something important to him: sailing. When he started sharing his weekend racing stories, others in the office began to see him less as a recluse and more as who he really was: a caring, hardworking man with a passion for sailing in his schooner with his family.

Bringing your authentic best self to every interaction both personally and professionally is at the core of competent bragging. For those who are reluctant to toot their own horn, this requires cultivating natural skills and qualities that have been buried or inhibited in the name of "acting" professional. As people bring more of themselves to an interaction, they are perceived as comfortable and relaxed, with an ease about them. When they acknowledge human feelings in their interactions with clients, customers, underlings, and superiors, they are seen as warm, caring, and empathic. Revealing carefully selected personal details about themselves makes others feel more comfortable in their presence. They speak at a moderate volume and maintain eye contact. They become part entertainer, part salesperson, and part educator. In a nutshell, by marrying their best personal style with their best material, they create lasting and memorable connections and impressions.

Brag Nag #3:
RECOGNIZE THE IMPORTANCE OF
FIRST IMPRESSIONS

There is one thing our parents were right about when it comes to first impressions: *Every* second counts. Communication research has shown that within the first one-thousandth of a second of meeting you, those on the receiving end have already started clicking off judgments about you. Within seven seconds, they're trying to determine whether they like and trust you, and whether you appear confident and qualified. If they can't decide within that time frame, they spend the next thirty to sixty seconds going through a critical checklist in their heads about you. Are you a potentially good hire? Do you have a command of your subject? Are you ready for that promotion? Do we really want you running our business or company? Are you worth talking to for the next ten minutes? Are you just full of hot air and overly impressed with yourself?

Most of us experience brag-fright, the anxiety that grips reluctant self-promoters, when faced with unfamiliar social situations where we are making a first impression. We fear being judged. We fear looking unprofessional. We fear sounding stupid. And most of all, we fear being thought of as braggarts! As a result, we get nervous and tend to shrink into ourselves, making ourselves as small and as invisible as possible. We bow our head. Our eyes dip down and we begin to look like we're talking to our feet. Our voice loses all life, shifting to a flat monotone or, as tension rises, to a squeaky pitch. We swallow our words as we race through what we have to say, just to get it over with. In doing so, we are transmitting a whole slew of nonverbal communication cues that can sink us in seconds.

In coaching thousands of people over the years, I have repeatedly observed that first impressions are based on the visual and vocal cues we transmit: clothing, personal grooming, a handshake, eye contact, posture, vocal intonation. One classic UCLA study showed that 55 percent of the message received by others is completely nonverbal and is conveyed through body language and facial animation. And yet, in my experience, 99.9 percent of the people I have trained fail to recognize the importance of their nonverbal communication when introducing themselves.

General Patton Goes Phil Donahue

Recently I coached a software consultant who thought that his communication style was informal and "very approachable." I asked him to make a one-minute introduction of himself and what he did for a living to a group of eight colleagues. What we saw was someone who was anything but informal. His body language was perfect for a West Point cadet; shoulders thrust back, legs astride, hands clasped behind his back. His voice was loud and clipped, and he looked directly at everyone in the group—only over their heads. When he saw the video feedback he was shocked. I worked with him on relaxing his posture, varying the tone and speed of his voice to sound more conversational, and looking at the people he was talking to. In an hour he went from being General Patton to Dr. Phil.

If you start out on the wrong foot, you spend valuable time trying to dig your way out of a bad impression. It's so much easier to begin by making others see you the way you want them to, spending the rest of your interaction focusing on them rather than worrying about what they are thinking of you. The sooner you learn to take control of those precious seven seconds, the better your interactions will be.

One More Time

Keep the following nonverbal cues in mind for use in whatever communication situation you find yourself in, and for effective bragging in particular. You've probably heard most of this advice before from your mother, but in case you were too busy rebelling, it bears repeating:

Smile. The quickest way to set a positive tone for any encounter is to smile. I don't mean a goofy Jerry Lewis or Jim Carrey grin, or one artificially plastered on your face like lipstick. I mean a warm and sincere smile that spreads out from your lips, lights up your face, and shines right through your eyes. Many of my clients are completely unaware of their facial expressions, walking around with a frown or scowl on their face. When I later ask them about it, they reply "Oh, no. Nothing's wrong." Remember, a smile is your most important facial expression. It draws people to you. It inspires confidence and understanding. In a flash, it can change someone's impression of you. It makes other people feel good. It makes you feel good! Let your smile work for you.

The Eyes Have It. When someone who is being introduced to me doesn't look at me, looks over my shoulder, or drops his gaze to the floor, all sorts of alarm bells sound. I think he is either terribly shy, lacks confidence, or just isn't interested in meeting me. One thing is for sure: He is oblivious to the impact his lack of eye contact is having on me. So this is my rule of thumb: When facing others, maintain eye contact approximately three to eight seconds per person. The smaller the group, the longer the gaze, but make sure it's not to the point of staring. Your eyes should naturally move away, but make sure they come back. If you want to excuse yourself, do so graciously. You should say "It was nice meeting you" or "I enjoyed the conversation," looking them in the eyes and, if you haven't done so already, extending a hearty handshake.

Good Posture. Your posture reflects your level of confidence and energy. Whether sitting, standing, walking the hallways, shaking hands, or giving a speech, people who believe they are successful carry themselves well. When we get nervous, most of us resort to one of two posture modes: either the rounded-shoulders "orangutan" look (yes, you've got the picture!), or the stiff and erect "Buckingham Palace changing of the guard" look. One thing I tell my clients is to think Jackie Onassis, who always looked like she had a taut string running from the center of her head to the ceiling. "Oh, is that what you mean?" they say, and instantly their shoulders shift back, their chest becomes wide, and they glide purposefully into the room with an air of grace, competence, and dignity that says "I believe in myself and what I have to say."

Voice. Confidence in yourself and what you're saying is also reflected in your voice. Your voice is the primary vehicle for conveying enthusiasm, interest, and setting a conversational tone, all the key ingredients of good bragging. Most men have the anatomical gift of natural vocal resonance and volume that works to their advantage. I coach them to sustain the same volume and tone, and to avoid mumbling or swallowing words at the end of their sentences. Women, on the other hand, can have all sorts of voice issues. Fearful of coming off as too big and powerful, they find that their voice often becomes softer, breathier, lighter, higher in pitch, resembling that of a little girl (or Marilyn Monroe) rather than that of an accomplished professional. They convert declarative statements into questions by ending sentences with an upward inflection. I instruct these women to inner-monologue the words *declare* and *convince* before they speak and then put their stake in the ground and say what it is they want to say with conviction and enthusiasm.

Dress. Your clothes are one of the first things people notice about you, and can be a way to project that you feel good about yourself. But when it comes to your career, how you dress also needs to be a strategic consideration.

For example, a friend of mine recently interviewed for a management position with a technology company in the Boston area. His wife, an investment banker, berated him for not wearing a conservative suit and tie. With dress codes in flux these days, she thought moving back to more traditional office attire would be safer. But he'd found after doing a little research that the technology company had a business-casual dress code, and he decided that a more formal suit would have, in fact, made him come across as stiff and even inexperienced. So he took his look one notch down, wearing a pair of khakis, business shirt opened at the collar, with a sport coat and loafers. It was a clean, comfortable, and professional look without going overboard.

I've always been a proponent of integrating your own style into business dress if you can pull it off and if it's appropriate. Many of my male Wall Street clients wear colorful suspenders and theme ties with their traditional suits. One woman I know works at a rather conservative law firm, but dresses in very colorful, feminine attire. One day, she walked into my office wearing a long skirt and a craft jacket in turquoise and blues, and she looked absolutely stunning. So why would I suggest that she wear dark suits and pearls when she radiates confidence in this outfit, and distinguishes herself with her unique wardrobe?

Personal Grooming. On the topic of good grooming, Dan Rather once remarked, "Never eat spinach just before going on the air." While you probably aren't facing millions of viewers each night, and many will forgive that sauce smudge on your cheek from the spareribs you just devoured at the corporate barbecue, it's nevertheless true that a good professional look is a clean and polished one. It makes a huge difference in how we are perceived by others. If people are fixated on the piece of spinach wedged between your teeth, they are never going to hear a word you say. Many believe that proper grooming simply requires bathing daily, shaving, wearing clean clothes, brushing your teeth, and combing your hair. That's good for starters, but don't overlook the finer details that can override even the pearliest whites.

For example, I noticed that one thirty-something marketing executive always seemed to have shiny metallic slivers around the bottom of her skirts. When I asked what they were, she replied, "Darn it! Can you really see them? I thought I had hidden those safety pins that were holding up my hem. I guess I'd better call my tailor!"

Brag Nag #4:
ACT LIKE YOUR BEST SELF
(EVEN WHEN YOU REALLY DON'T FEEL LIKE IT)

Often we find ourselves in situations we would rather not be in that take us out of our comfort zone. We've worked all night and feel exhausted, but face a long day with an important client; we have to attend an annual corporate holiday party when we'd rather be home with our children; we've been asked on short notice to fill in for our boss who can't make it to a critical meeting with senior management; we haven't successfully landed a job and are dispirited facing yet another networking event.

What do we do? We rise to the occasion; we *act like* our best self. This doesn't mean we act like someone we are not, just that we stay in touch with how we would behave if we were genuinely delighted to be there.

Under the Weather

You've got a fever of 102. The phone rings and your assistant tells you that the chairman of your advertising agency has just called and needs to see you in her New York office tomorrow afternoon.

If you were really being frank, you would say, "Tell Ms. Chairman I have a terrible cold, my head hurts, my nose is running nonstop, and to make matters worse, I had a terrible fight with my husband last night." Chances are, however, you will pull yourself together, get out of bed, book the next flight, graciously meet with Ms. Chairman, listen attentively, contribute enthusiastically, and act like you are delighted to be there. "Oh, this little cold?" you might reply when Ms. Chairman inquires about your bright red nose, as you pull tissue after tissue from the compact floral holder, adding, "It's nothing, really." You act as you do when you feel well and rested. In other words, you act like your best self.

We transmit our best self by acting as if we want to be there. Here's a simple behavioral technique that can help you act as if. I call it Over the Top (OTT) and it works like this: Recite silently, or aloud, situation permitting, a number of monologue phrases (listed below) in a very exaggerated manner. Practice them with the zeal of a televangelist. You will probably feel silly and uncomfortable at first, but when your best self is deflated from fever, insecurity, or brag-fright, nothing helps you slip back into your most confident, competent, and persuasive self faster than practicing OTT.

- I am so happy to be here!
- I can't wait to tell you about me!
- You're not going to believe this!
- Wait until you hear this one!
- Sit down and listen!
- I have fabulous news!

Clients find going Over the Top tremendously helpful because nine times out of ten when they use it, genuine enthusiasm and delight follow. This technique recognizes, as effective self-promoters know, that people like to be around people who are upbeat. It's fine to make occasional note of your personal problems and, as work crisscrosses more with our personal lives, it's a natural thing to do. But someone who whines constantly about crises and problems becomes irritating even to the most forgiving friends and business acquaintances.

Brag Nag #5:
CONVEY EXCITEMENT ABOUT YOUR WORK
AND ACCOMPLISHMENTS

People want to listen to others who are excited about who they are, what they do, and what they are saying. Unfortunately, many associate enthusiasm with being unprofessional. One client told me, "Peggy, I'm an engineer. I'm supposed to be boring!" I've heard this excuse from people in every field. Their thinking goes something like this: If I get too excited, that means I'm getting too emotional, and that means that I'm getting too subjective, and that means facts fly out the window, along with my credibility.

Nothing could be further from the truth. There is no rule that says an expert has to be boring. Enthusiasm breeds enthusiasm. Confidence breeds confidence.

Often at the beginning of my workshops, I travel around the room asking audience members to stand up, introduce themselves, and briefly describe what they do and where they went to college. At a recent gathering of women in investment banking, I selected three women, all beautifully groomed and dressed, who were at about the same level in their respective jobs. Here were their responses:

"My name is Joanne. I'm a vice president who works in banking helping multimillion-dollar companies manage their accounts. I am a graduate of Yale, with a master's in business from Stanford."

"My name is Beatrice. I'm a vice president who specializes in money management for large public institutions. I am also the mother of two wonderful kids. I got my degree from Princeton."

"My name is Rhonda. I'm not an Ivy Leaguer. I attended Arizona State University and got a degree in anthropology. But that hasn't stopped me. I'm a vice president in private banking with a specialty in wealth management. I work individually with everyone, from people with family trusts to those who, after years of hard work, suddenly hit payday when they reach the top of their organizations, sell their companies, or go IPO. The best part of what I do is watching people finally get there!"

When I later asked the group who they wanted to know more about, everyone named Rhonda. Why? She had a sense of urgency, an excitement about her work. She actually seemed delighted to be telling us her story, even turning her potential weak spots into strengths. She came off as being so genuine that everyone wanted to get to know her better. As one woman said, "Believe me, the moment I hit pay dirt, I'm calling Rhonda."

Brag Nag #6:
SCHMOOZE!

A lot of business people hate schmoozing. While Leo Rosten's *Joys of Yiddish* defines it as a friendly, heart-to-heart talk, people perceive it as superficial or even manipulative chatter that one is forced to engage in at social events.

They fail to see schmoozing as an ideal way to market themselves.

Let me make one thing perfectly clear: Good schmoozers are *not* con artists. They are superb conversationalists who take the time to connect with others, whether it's around the office watercooler, at a cocktail party, networking at an industry event, at a meeting, pitching new business, or interviewing for a job. Effective schmoozing is a sincere exchange of experiences and ideas that help people develop rapport and intimacy with each other. Most people in their business communication, however, don't take the time, energy, and creativity to schmooze. They have the tendency to fall back on a communication style that has its underpinnings in Presentation 101. They "agendize." They dump information, reciting fact after boring fact instead of weaving the information into a pithy, entertaining story that gets their message across. They proceed to engage in a one-way soliloquy and get sucked into the sinkhole of mediocrity. If they show their humanness, they believe, no one will take them seriously. They avoid preliminary chitchat; it's more efficient to get to the business at hand and keep the discussion focused and on track rather than getting to know and personally relating to others. All of these characteristics make for uninspired and lackluster self-promoters.

Effective interpersonal communication is a two-way, back-and-forth, interactive affair. If by chance you've forgotten how it works, it goes like this: You acknowledge someone, she acknowledges you. You say something, she listens and says something back to. You listen and respond, perhaps posing a question; the other person listens and says something back to you. And the cycle repeats itself—you have a conversation! If you engage others thoughtfully, you schmooze. Good schmoozers talk to people as if they really mattered. They listen carefully and draw people out. They look for common ground. They ask people what they do or what they've been up to. They remember names and make mental notes of important details: children, lifestyle, favorite hobbies and interests, even a sore back. They seem genuinely interested in what others have to say. And then, when the timing is right, they take the opportunity to seamlessly plant positive seeds about themselves—their background, accomplishments, interests, passions, and projects they are working on—in a meaningful and measured way.

"But . . . if you're good at what you do, won't your work speak for itself?"

That's all well and good if someone's listening, but these days, in the age of information overload, mergers, and merry-go-round management, you can't assume anything. Remember, other people don't get up in the morning thinking, "What can I do for you?"

Self-Serving Is for Cafeterias Only

There's a guy I know named Warren whom I've started to avoid because he has forgotten how to schmooze. Every time he sees me, he launches into some kind of name-dropping, self-congratulatory spew, before I've had the chance to ask about how he's doing, or before he's asked me how I am.

"Peggy!" he shouts upon spotting me. Racing up to me, he says, "You won't believe all the great things that have been happening to me. You know how scared I was a couple of months ago about going off on my own? Well, I have gotten every piece of business I've gone after, and they are all Fortune 500 companies. I mean really big players! Actually, there really aren't that many people out there who can do what I do, 'cause if there were, for sure these guys would have hired them. I mean, you can't take away a happy customer, can you? And, listen, it would be great if you would throw me a few of your clients to call so that I can really get filled up for the summer. I'm sure they need someone like me to help them out in their operations. I gotta run. I'll call you next week."

It's clear that Warren is not really interested in my life; he's just trying to impress me and get referrals—a complete turnoff. If he schmoozed and engaged in some preliminary chitchat, if he talked with me, not at me, and wove in his accomplishments naturally, it would be much easier for me to converse with him. Instead, he sounds like one of those annoying telemarketers calling at dinnertime. What's worse, he's a repeat offender; he does this every single time I see him. He is forever trying to prove himself, which makes him look even more insecure, self-serving, and superficial. Good braggers know better. They see schmoozing as a gateway to stronger personal relationships and opportunities for better self-promotion.

A Schmoozer Connects

In business we've all been taught to begin a presentation or discussion with "Today, I'm here to speak with you about . . ." Let me ask you something. If you take a friend out for a cup of coffee, do you sit down and announce, "Today, I want to talk to you about . . ." and proceed to give him a bulleted agenda of what you're about to say? Instead, you might start off with "It's good to see you"; "How are you?"; or "Coming over here today, I heard a joke on the radio I thought you'd appreciate." Then you might subtly give him a general roadmap of what you need to cover with him. Effective schmoozers never agendize; they conversationalize all forms of speech. And it doesn't matter whether they are facing one, five, or five thousand. They always seem as if they are having an intimate conversation with each person in the room.

One of the great public schmoozers is Scott McNealy, chairman and CEO of Sun Microsystems. Listening to his 2001 speech to the National Press Club on the economy and his company's future, it was hard to tell he was standing on a podium and facing a roomful of journalists. With his ease of verbal expression, a dry wit, and the casual mention of personal details, he could just as easily have been sitting in his living room having a one-to-one chat.

Thank you for the introduction, Bill. I guess when you come to the press club they do research on you. You're telling me stuff I didn't even remember. It was pretty accurate [pause] in some areas. Glad to hear, too, that this is all off the record today. Right? [The group of journalists bursts into laughter.] Just kidding. I guarantee that you'll get plenty of content here. They'd like me to talk for twenty to twenty-five minutes so I've got forty to forty-five topics I'd like to race through. But I'll do three things. I'd like to put a disclaimer on what I'm about to say; we are in pretty interesting economic times, so I'd also like to talk about that on a macro level, and then show you some product demos of some new technologies. I'm a golf major, so don't worry, I won't get too technical for a lot of you, so you don't have to bolt early. Here's my disclaimer: What do I know? There are a lot of people who worry and work and think about the national and political and economic decisions and situations way more than I do. I have a full day job and three boys in car seats, so I'm fully employed . . .

Brag Nag #7:
TAKE THE EMOTIONAL TEMPERATURE
OF YOUR LISTENERS

What made Scott McNealy so effective in his opening remarks? He took the emotional temperature of his listeners and customized his message accordingly. In less than ninety seconds, he acknowledged they were in the news business and hence, short on time and in need of real news. (*Translation: Stick around and you'll get what you need.*) He recognized that many were not technically savvy. (*Translation: You won't have to sit through a bunch of technobabble, so be sure to stay long enough to see our new product demos.*) He poked fun at them with his "off the record" remark. (*Translation: I know how you guys work, for better or worse.*) In a self-deprecating way, he set up the fact that he wasn't an economist, but a businessman speaking from his own experience and observations in running a successful public company. (*Translation: Take my economic forecasts with a grain of salt.*) He then showed his humanity with reference to his three young sons and his golf game. (*Translation: I'm human like you. Have mercy.*)

So for better bragging, first set the stage by asking yourself, regardless of whether you're standing in front of one or many: Who's my audience? What are their goals, needs, and objectives? What thoughts and feelings have they come into the room with: eagerness, frustration, anger, or fear? What issues do they have with me? What will reinforce trust in our relationship? If you are preoccupied with presenting a perfect image to the world, you project so much self-absorption that you miss important opportunities to connect with others.

Getting Carried Away with PowerPoint

These days Microsoft PowerPoint is all the rage for preparing and presenting information to groups of people. As its popularity has risen, many people have come to believe that whenever they are in front of a group, they need to whip out their PowerPoint. If they stopped and really reflected on the true needs of their audience, they might find that is not always the case.

Recently the president of a large advertising firm, a longtime friend of mine, described his preparations for a prelaunch sales and marketing meeting with the publishing house that was soon to be releasing his first book. He kept emphasizing the importance of getting his Power-Point presentation "just right" for the twenty people from various departments who would be in the meeting. As we talked about his plans, he casually mentioned that his agent, a mutual friend, was against his using PowerPoint because she thought it was more important for him to establish a personal relationship with the members of the publishing team than to present a bunch of factual information. The agent wanted him to bring only himself, as he had at their initial proposal meetings with editors when, as she put it, he wowed them with his personality, demeanor, and expertise. She thought that our friend would be better served at the upcoming meeting by informally discussing the sales and marketing strategy and by building a rapport with the key players who were going to be so essential to the book's success.

In the end, even with my objections added to his agent's, Mr. President took his twenty-five-slide Power-Point presentation to the meeting. Later he hinted to me that maybe we were right after all. When I asked the agent what happened, she said, "I couldn't believe that he pulled out that PowerPoint presentation. When he was on the fifth slide, I looked out and saw a sea of glazed stares. Sensing the downward direction of the meeting, I said, 'You know, I don't think we need to see all of this right now; let's just talk. What does the publicity department have in mind?' Everyone proceeded to join in the discussion. In the end, they all connected the way they should have in the first place."

The way we talk, listen, and respond to others will strongly influence how they respond to us. We all want to feel that we are being personally acknowledged. When we believe that someone is truly addressing our feelings and intentions, we respect him and feel more open to what he has to say. Talk and listen with your whole body: your eyes, your ears, your head, and your heart.

Brag Nag #8:
LEVERAGE THE POWER OF HUMOR, STORIES, AND ANECDOTES

What is the single most memorable, impressive, and credible way to reveal yourself and your accomplishments in an unassuming and magically invisible manner? Tell a story about yourself in a colorful, lighthearted, or humorous way. Everybody loves a story, and we all have lots of them. When used as a bragging tool, a story can engage people and allow you to subtly sing your own praises in a way that comes off as authentic but disarming. Using real-life anecdotes to show how you've solved problems, how you got interested in your field, what makes you just right for the job, or simply describe what you do for a living is a more powerful and compelling way of expressing yourself than stating the facts will ever be. Unlike those reasoned facts, a story well told will set you apart from the competition.

Recently I was helping the managing director of a large investment firm craft a pitch on the importance of teamwork—in which she had to demonstrate her leadership capabilities—for delivery to a postmerger group of sixty employees in her newly formed division. She opened by saying:

> I've come from Wall Street, where the mentality is "every man for himself," to a firm that is quite different in the sense that teamwork is directly linked to compensation. In fact, your bonuses are completely tied to the collective efforts and successes of this team. I actually know a lot more about teamwork than you might suspect. Long before I started my career, I grew up in a family with seven children. I was number five. I learned very quickly that there can be multiple views on even the simplest of topics, from whose turn it was to do the dishes or mow the lawn to where to go on our next vacation—believe me, with seven kids packed in a car on a cross-country journey, it was important that everyone was happy with the decision! Essentially, for things to run smoothly we all had to march to the same beat. So I am here today to offer my views on what I think our goals and objectives should be, and most important, to get input from each and every one of you over the course of the next two weeks.

Personal stories and anecdotes, injected with a bit of humor when appropriate, are your most powerful tools in learning how to brag without backlash. When they illustrate a relevant or important point, they can help you avoid coming off like you're talking about yourself just for the sake of talking about yourself, the hallmark of irritating braggers. They allow you to bond with those who are listening to you and communicate more effectively while subtly underscoring your history and strong points. Okay, so enough nagging. Start bragging!

CHAPTER 10

————————◎————————

A Confession and
Twelve Tooting Tips

I'd like to leave you with a confession and twelve tooting tips for mastering the art of bragging. First the confession.

Early on in my coaching career I was in Santa Fe to give a workshop on executive presence to a group of female physicians. These women were incredibly bright and accomplished, with multiple degrees and specialties I couldn't even pronounce. When I arrived at the check-in table, I was handed a badge that said "Peggy Klaus, Communication Expert." I was horrified. How could I possibly walk around and so brazenly pronounce myself *expert*? I ran back to my hotel room and worked feverishly at rubbing the word off the badge, only succeeding in erasing the *T.* When I stood up that morning in front of the group of distinguished women, I decided to begin the workshop by telling this story.

After being introduced, I shook my head and started to laugh, saying:

The most incredible thing just happened to me that I think all of you can relate to. This morning I came down to the registration desk, where they handed me a badge that said "Peggy Klaus, Communication Expert." I grabbed the badge and ran upstairs to my room, where I started to hyperventilate while dialing my husband at work. "Oh my God, Randy," I blurted out to him when he picked up the phone. I sounded so upset that he thought I had been in an accident and was calling from a hospital. "They gave me this badge at the conference that says 'Peggy Klaus, Communication Expert.'" There was dead silence before he asked, "And your point is?" I responded by saying that I couldn't possibly wear a badge proclaiming me as the expert, it's so obnoxious; it's so self-aggrandizing. Randy replied, "But you *are* the communication expert! That's why they've asked you to the conference." "Well, maybe," I said, adding, "but I can't have it say so on my badge."

"So what are you going to do?"

"I don't know," I said. "I have to be on stage in ten minutes. What would you do?"

"I would put on the badge, walk around proudly, and introduce myself to everyone by saying, 'Hi I'm Randy Keyworth, Communication Expert.'"

"You're no help!" I told him and hung up.

So what did I do? I picked up my butter knife off the room-service tray from breakfast and tried to rub out the word *expert* from my badge. But I only had five minutes before I needed to be downstairs and all I could get off was the letter *T.* So now I stand before you as Peggy Klaus, Communication Exper. And even though each of us in this room is an expert, we never think we are good enough. We suffer from the Impostor Complex. Even though I have successfully coached hundreds of clients, even though I've worked extensively with doctors on their teaching skills and bedside manner, even though I am published, even though I am totally educated and qualified, I still fear being caught not knowing everything a *real* expert in my field would know.

Before I could continue, the entire room was on its feet, applauding and cheering me on. When the room calmed, several women stood up and started to talk about their own similar experiences in the field of medical science. With my little confession I had relaxed this group of women doctors and formed a deep bond by relating to them personally. I had revealed my own vulnerability as a person and had shown the courage to expose my humanness. As you can see from the above, my presentation was 95 percent story and 5 percent tooting. But the subtle manner in which I conveyed my expert qualifications—in the context of an amusing, self-deprecating story—was infinitely more powerful and memorable than the path that ineffective and irritating tooters often take.

I have journeyed from a reluctant self-promoter to an artful one. Yet even today, I can still hear my father cautioning me to never toot my own horn. So whether you are far along in your career or just starting out, don't let your own bragging myths silence you. Self-promotion is undeniably a must-have skill in today's workplace. And as with anything else, the more you practice, the more adept you will become at selling yourself.

As you embark on your campaign, always remember that bragging is an art. Put a horn in the hands of someone who doesn't know how to toot and what do you hear? A cacophony that makes people turn away. Put it in the hands of someone who knows how to play, and it's music to the ears. When you learn to play your horn well, people will listen. And so it is with the art of bragging.

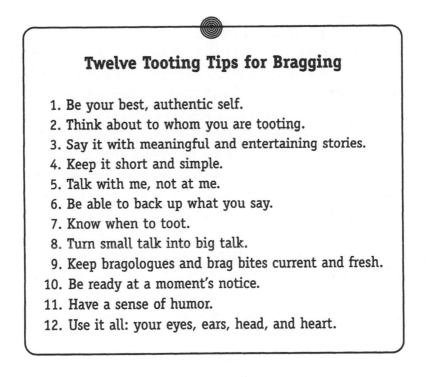

Twelve Tooting Tips for Bragging

1. Be your best, authentic self.
2. Think about to whom you are tooting.
3. Say it with meaningful and entertaining stories.
4. Keep it short and simple.
5. Talk with me, not at me.
6. Be able to back up what you say.
7. Know when to toot.
8. Turn small talk into big talk.
9. Keep bragologues and brag bites current and fresh.
10. Be ready at a moment's notice.
11. Have a sense of humor.
12. Use it all: your eyes, ears, head, and heart.

We would love to hear about
your bragging successes and bragging bombs.
Please visit our website
at *www.bragbetter.com*
for details on submitting your stories.

FOR YOUR NEXT EVENT . . . THINK BRAG!

- Professional Development
- Sales Training
- Orientations
- Annual Meetings
- And more . . .

BRAG! training content is broad-based, building skills for both professional development (promoting yourself and your agenda) and business development (promoting your company and its products). Programs range from a two-hour BRAG! Party (a cocktail-style networking event) to a two-day workshop. All BRAG! trainings are interactive and full of experiential exercises. They include opportunities for giving and receiving feedback, creating an elevator-pitch bragologue, and learning the skills needed to become a more dynamic communicator in all situations.

BRAG! Parties: Highly interactive, cocktail-style affairs, where people can network personally and professionally, and fearlessly practice tooting their own horns without blowing it. Klaus reveals key self-promotion techniques interspersed with fun, experiential exercises like speed bragging, where people change partners every few minutes.

BRAG! Workshops: An entertaining and informative way of reminding professionals about the critical importance of self-promotion in today's dog-eat-dog world, while giving them an opportunity to test Klaus's techniques for better bragging. Workshops extend the focus from promoting yourself to promoting your company's products and services. They can be scheduled for two hours to two days.

BRAG! Keynotes: Klaus offers BRAG! Keynote presentations that incorporate the interactive nature of her workshops and parties into a format appropriate for larger groups.

BRAG! CONNECTIONS Corporate Outreach: Offering companies and organizations the opportunity to build positive relationships with employees and consumers of the future, this cross-generational program expands the popular BRAG! lineup by pairing aspiring teens with seasoned workers to learn critical networking and self-promotion job skills. Find out more about bragging for teens at www.brag4teens.com.

The Hard Truth About Soft Skills: What's the hard truth? Soft skills—such as getting along with others, solving problems, and self promotion—get little respect, but can make or break your career. Yet unfortunately, most people learn them the hard way! Take Klaus's quick online self-assessment quiz at www.peggyklaus.com to help you identify your strengths and where you need improvement in the soft skills arena.

For more information about Klaus and her programs, visit our Web site at www.peggyklaus.com or call Klaus & Associates at 510-464-5921.